I0511153

Whales Coloring Book For Adults

This book belongs to:

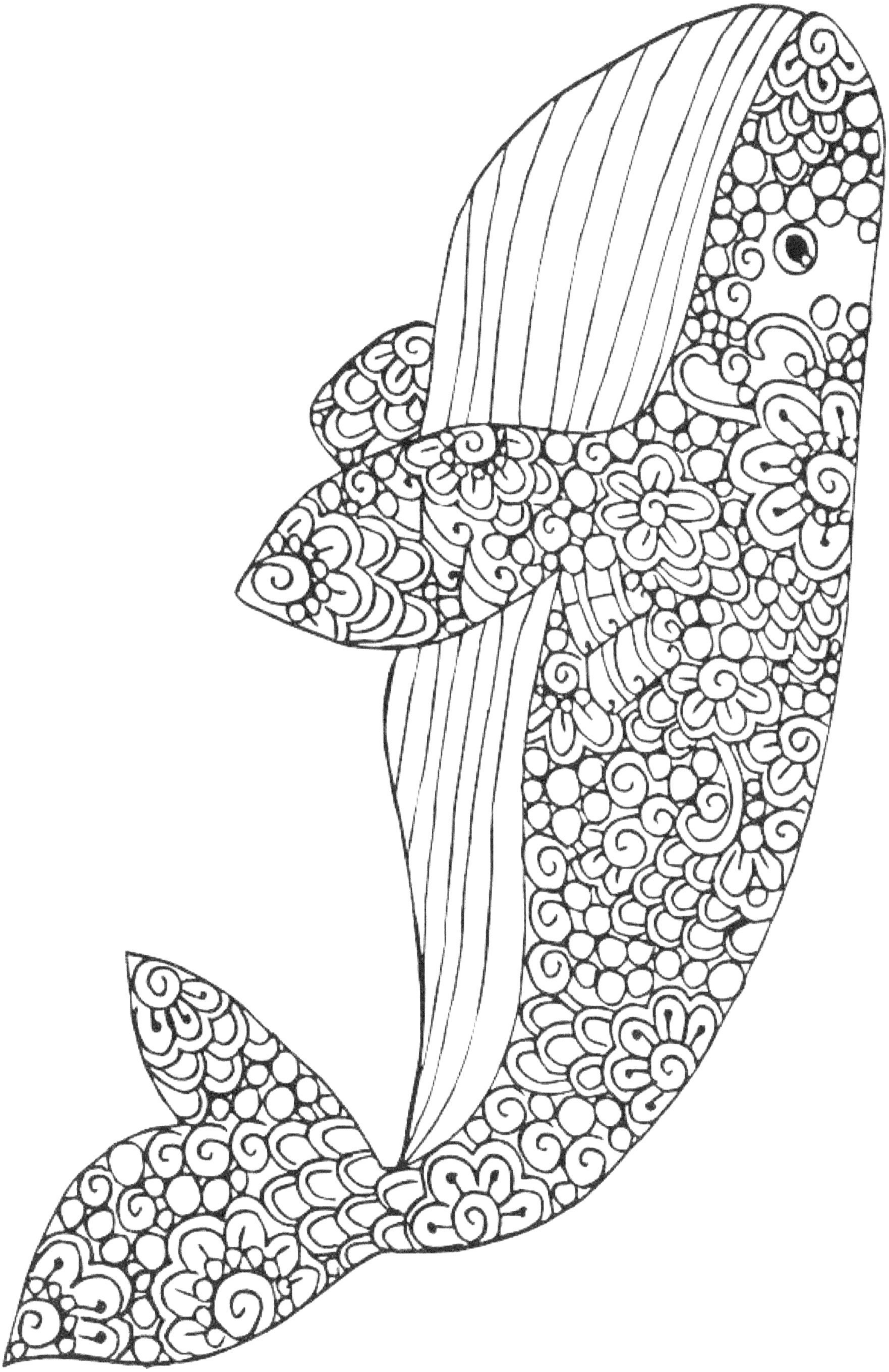

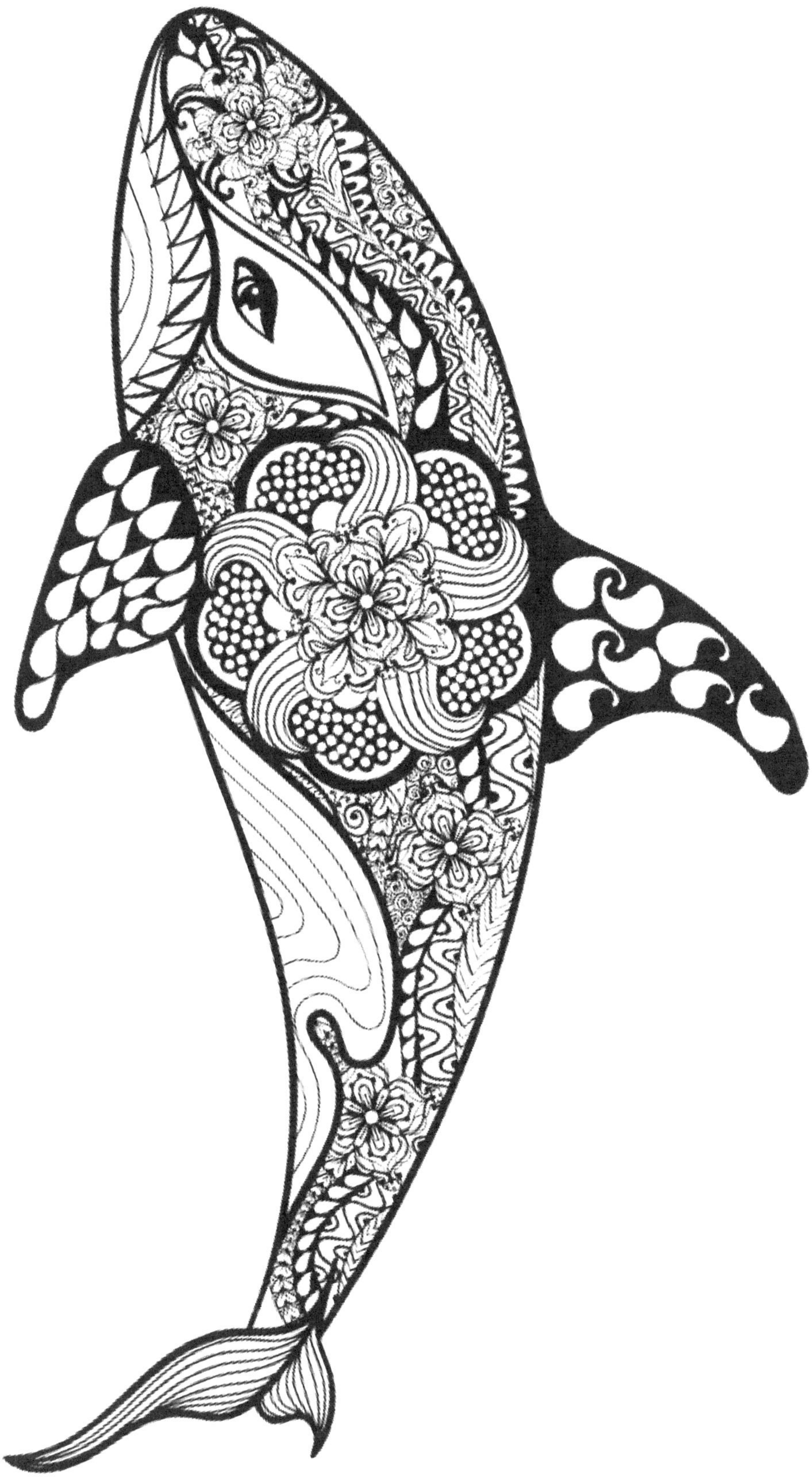

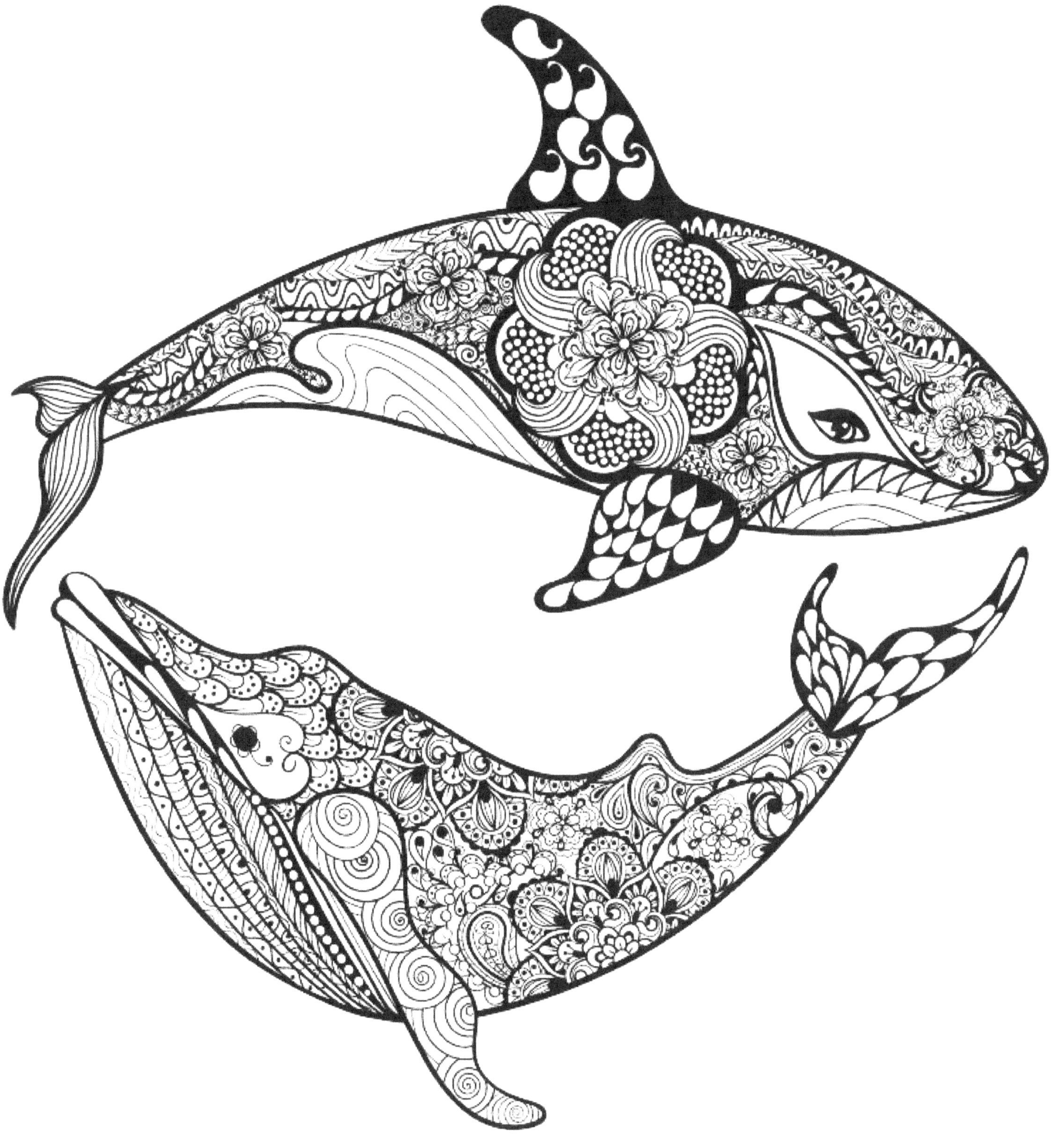

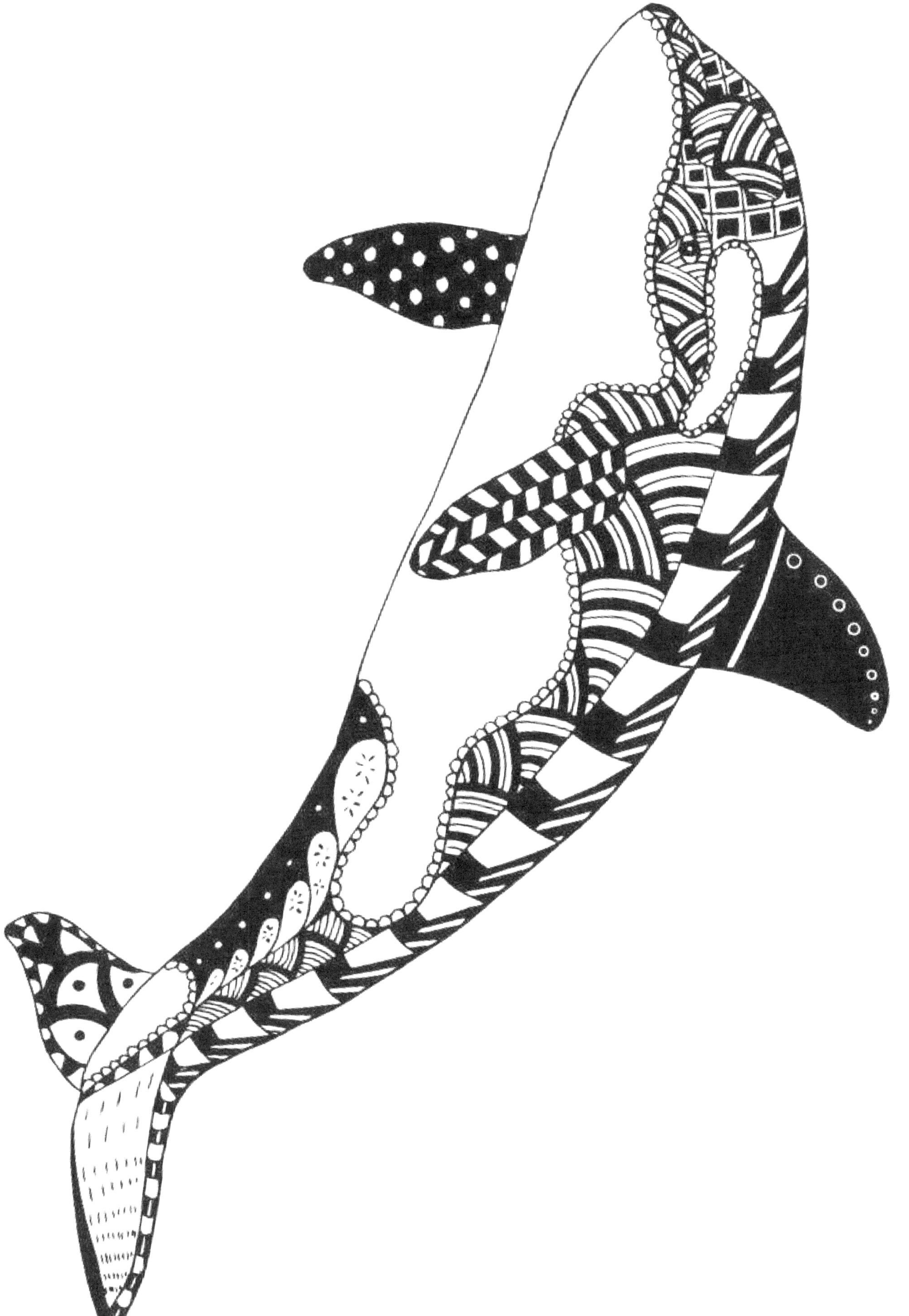

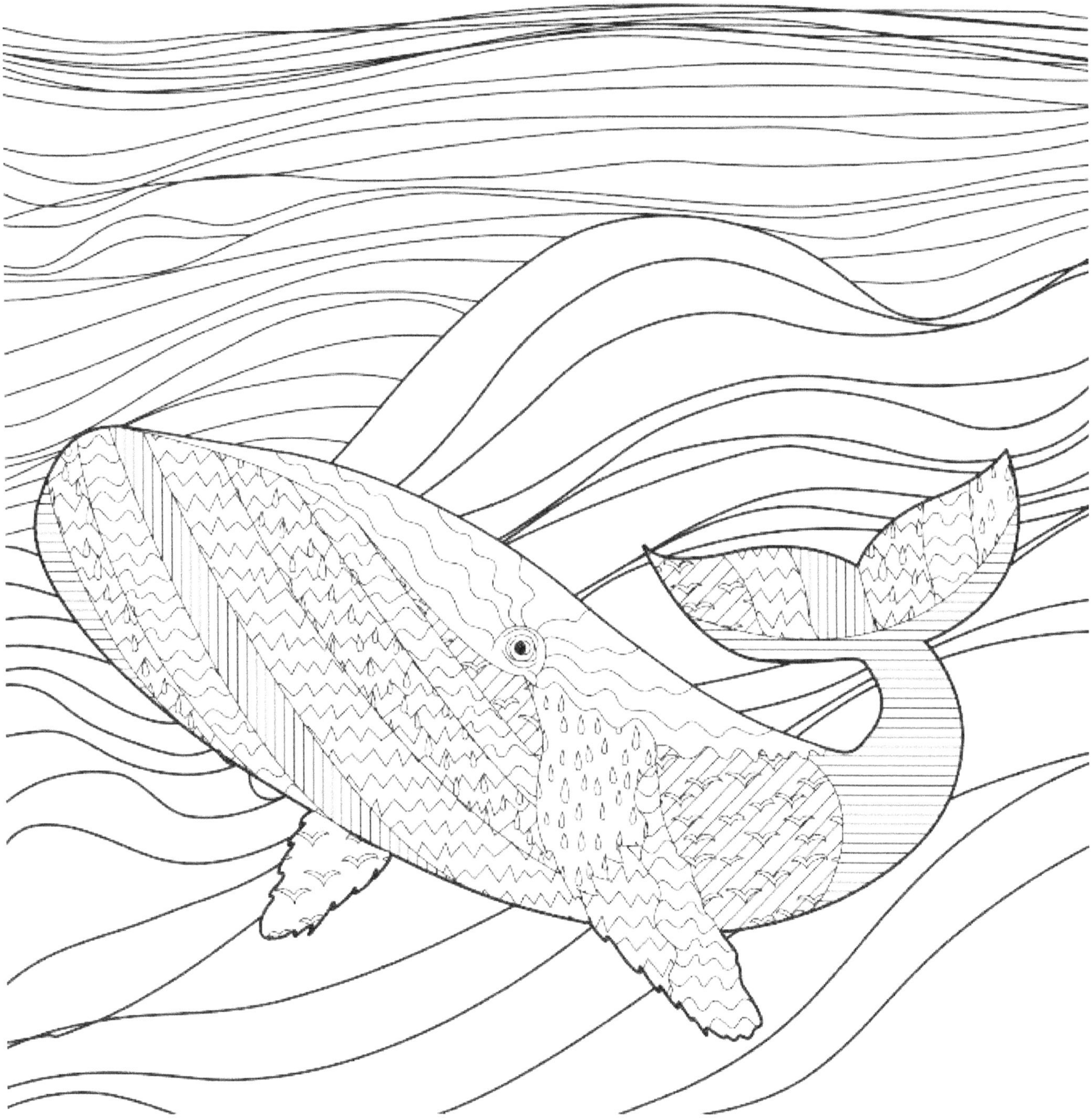

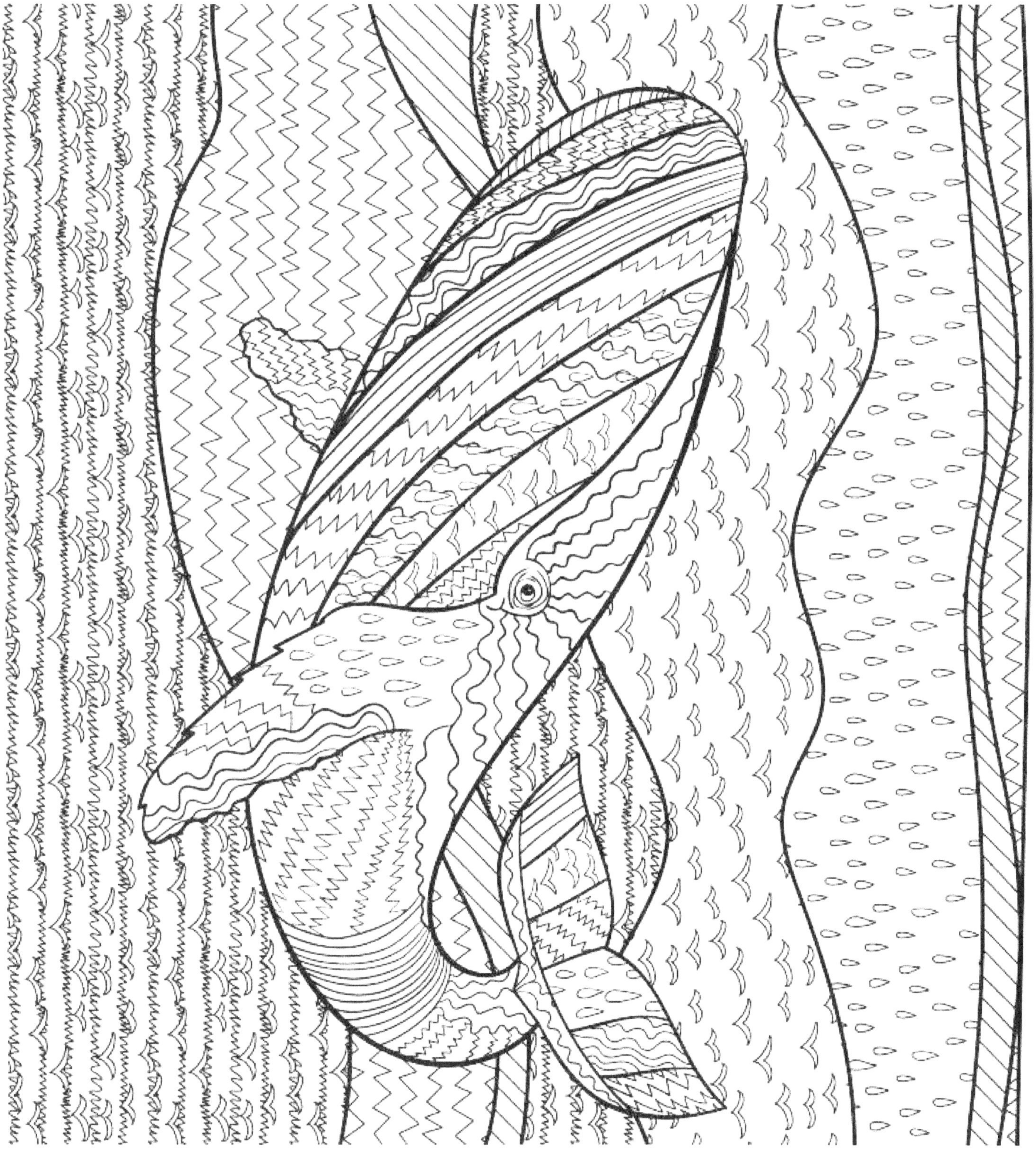

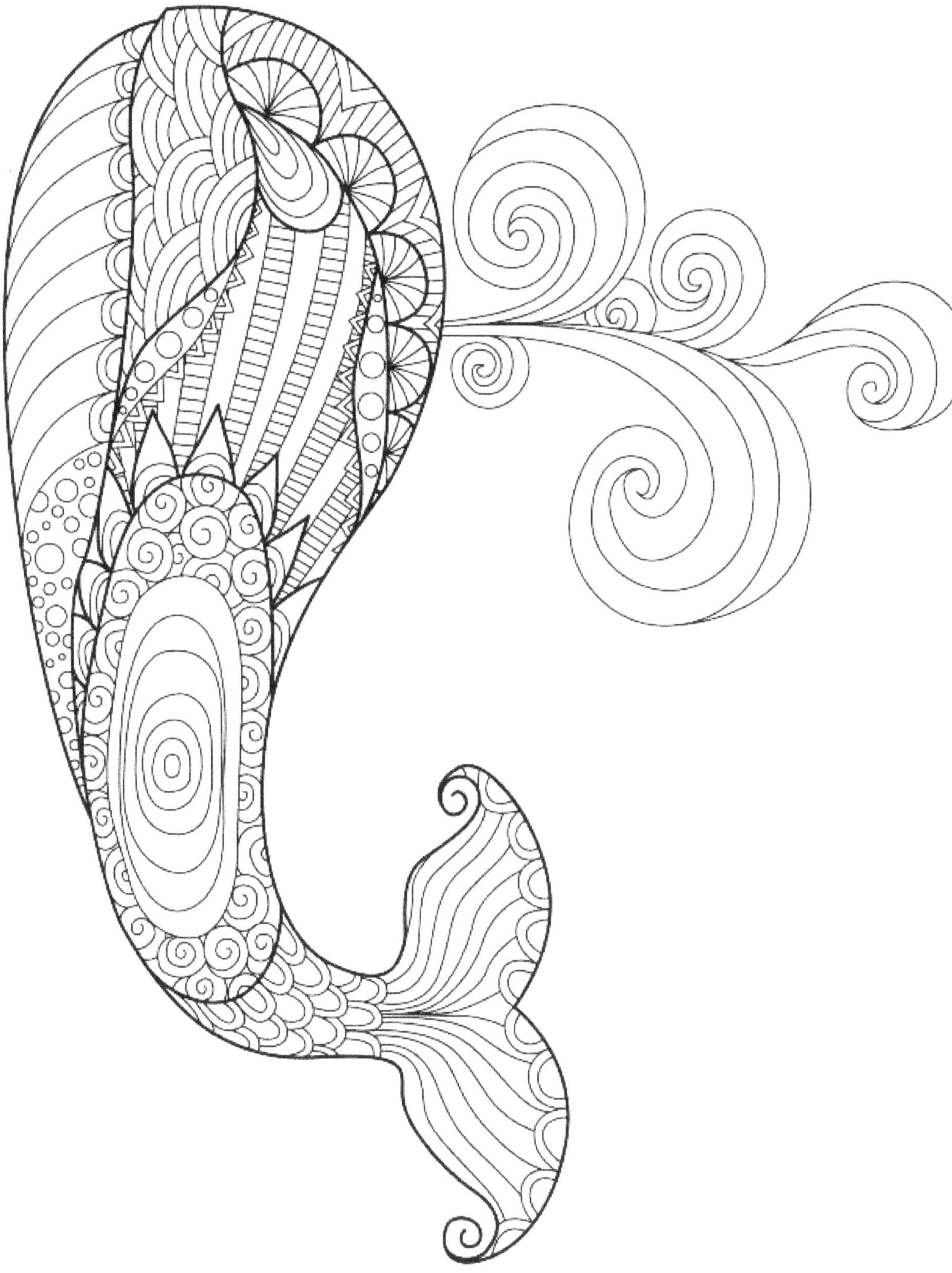

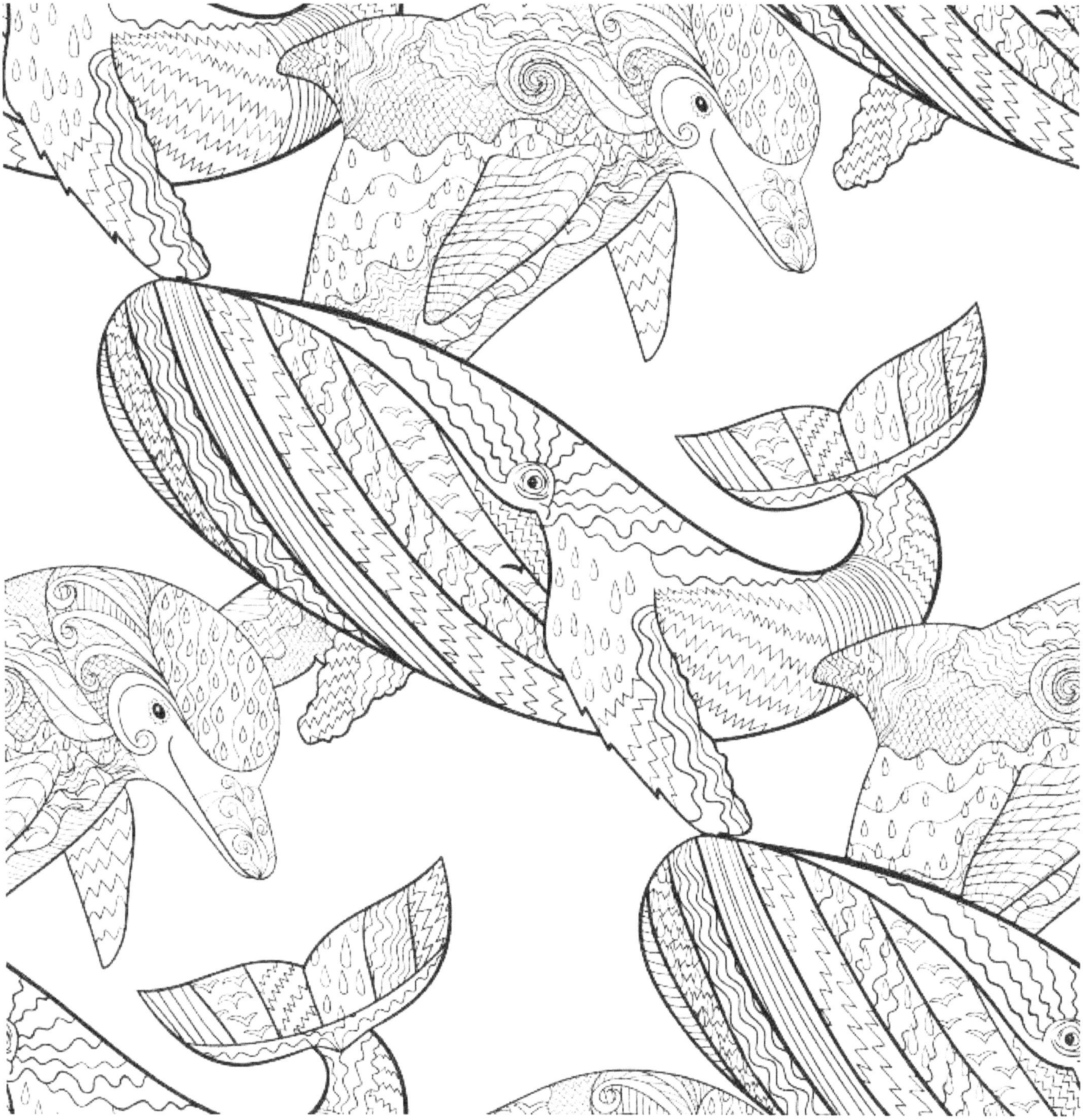

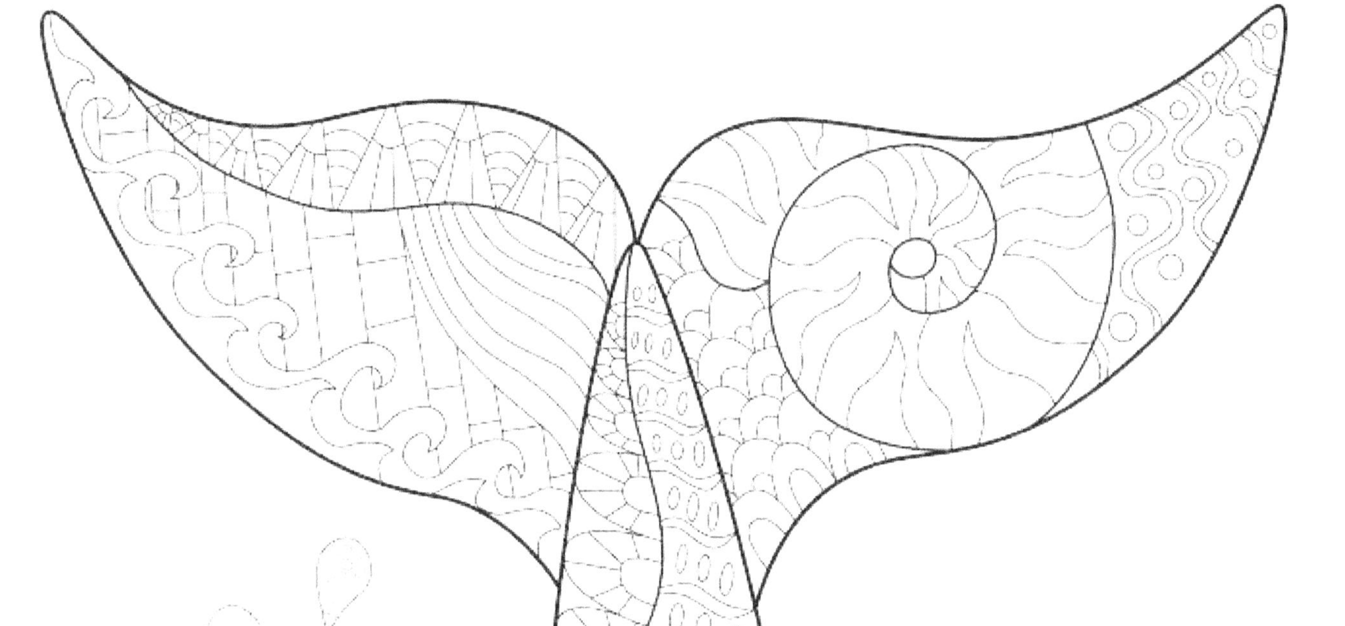

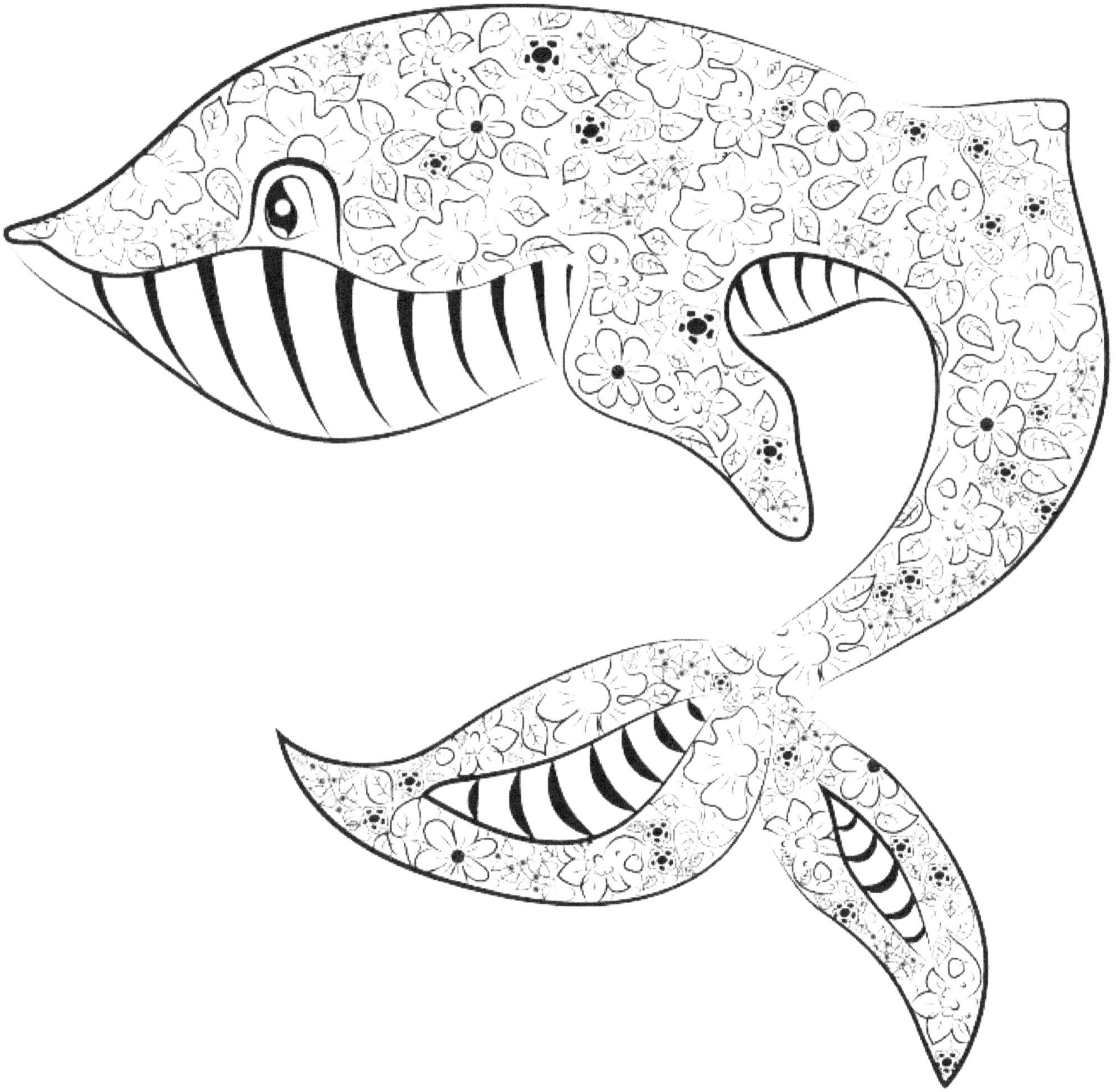

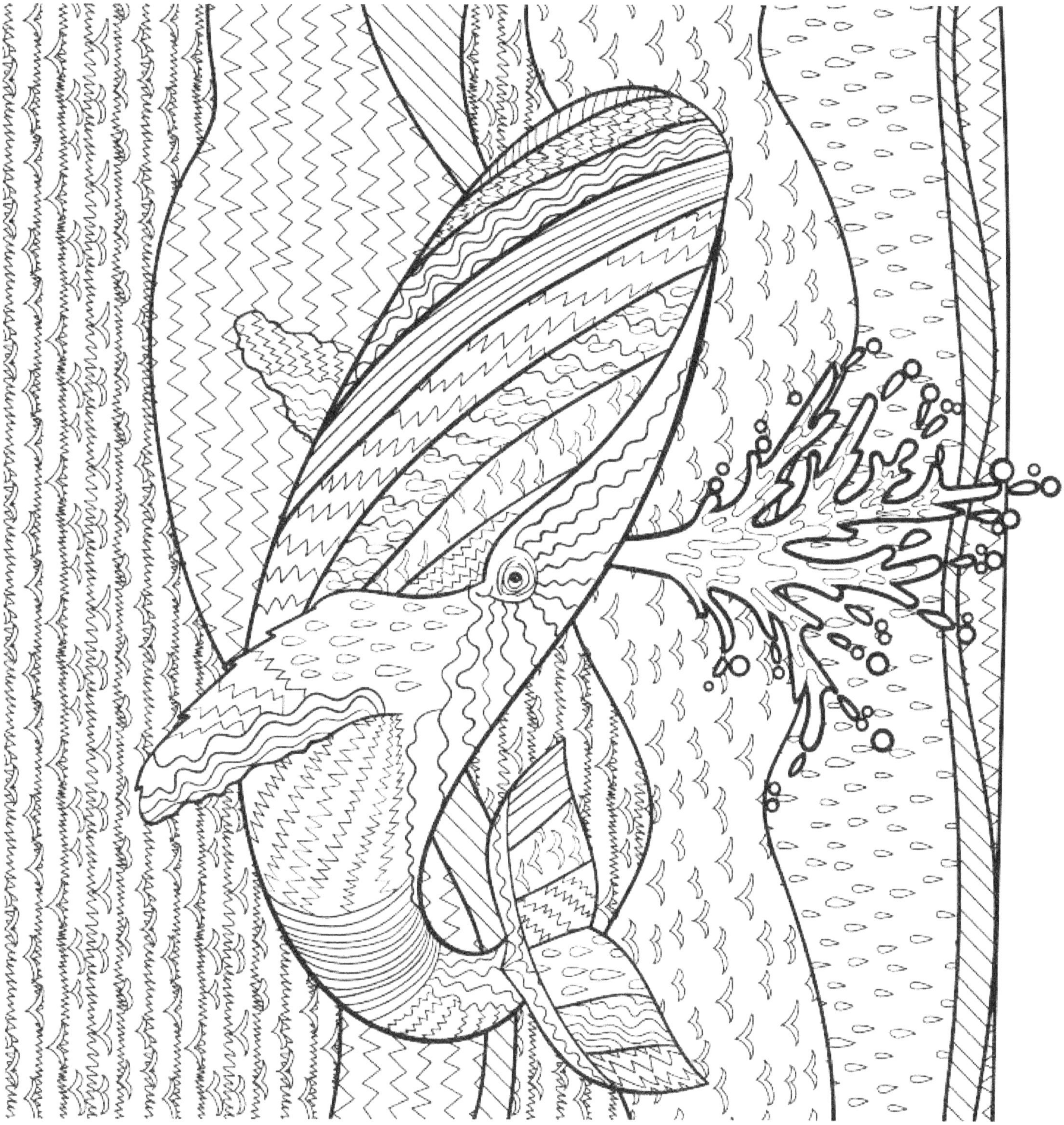

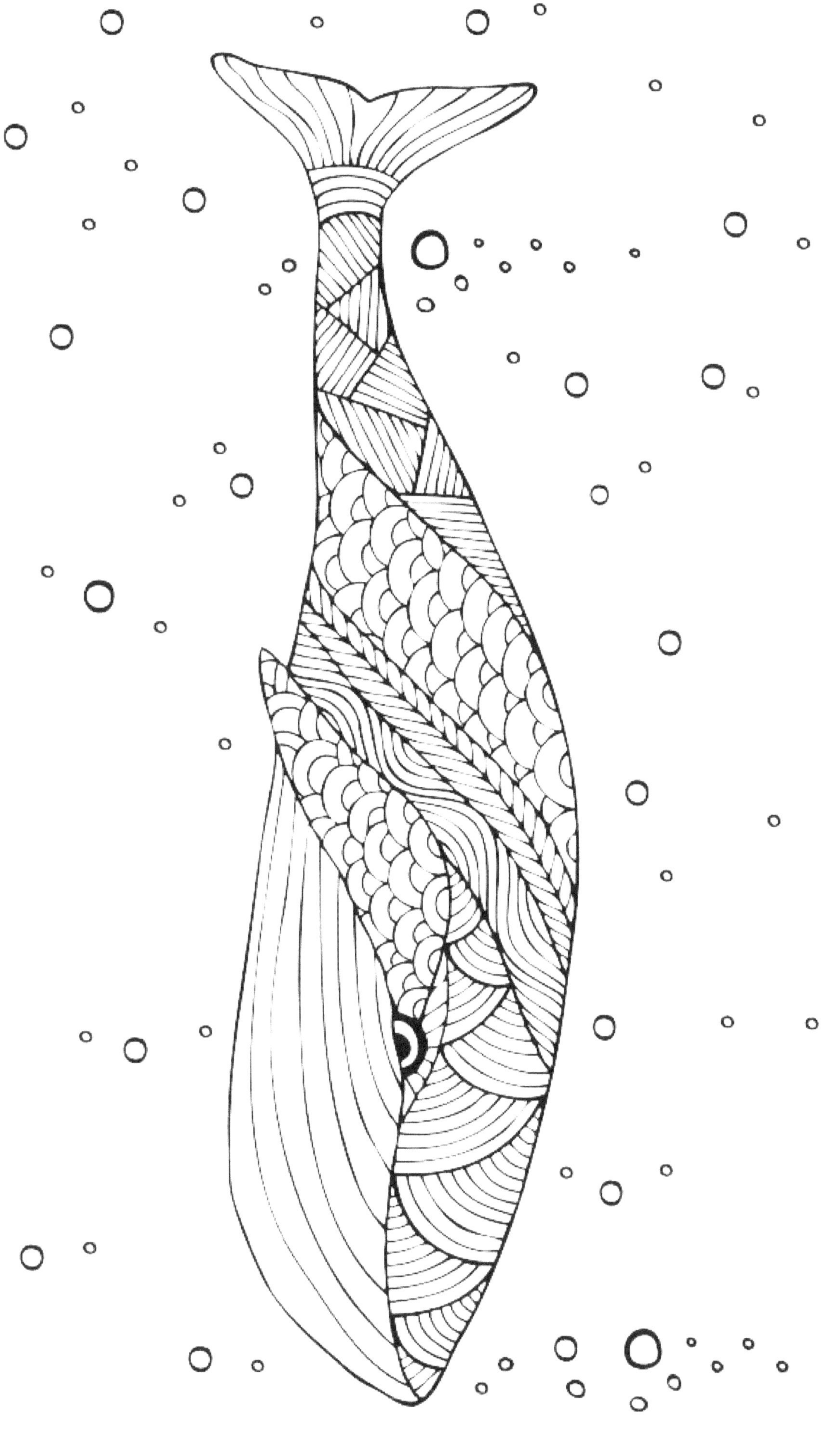

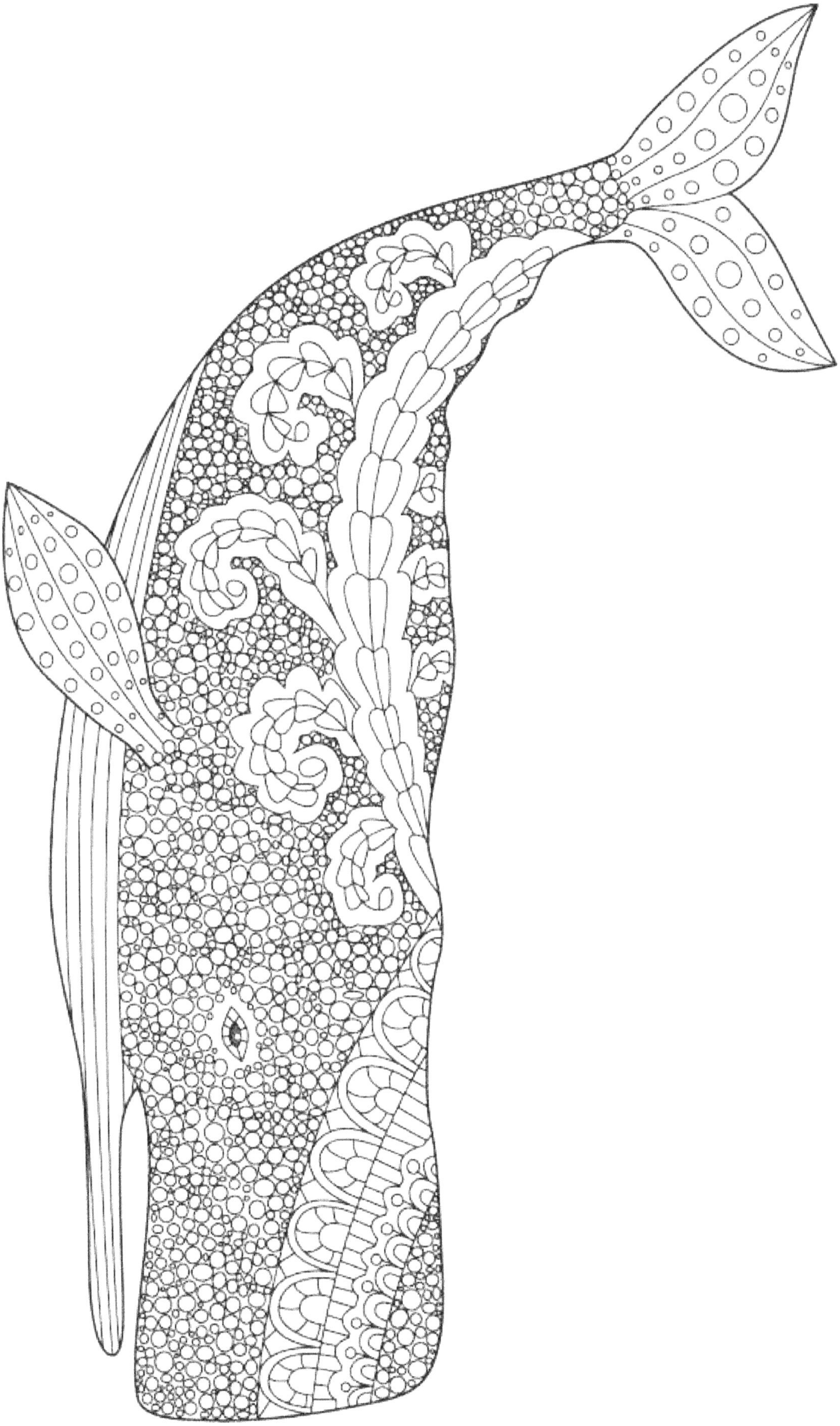

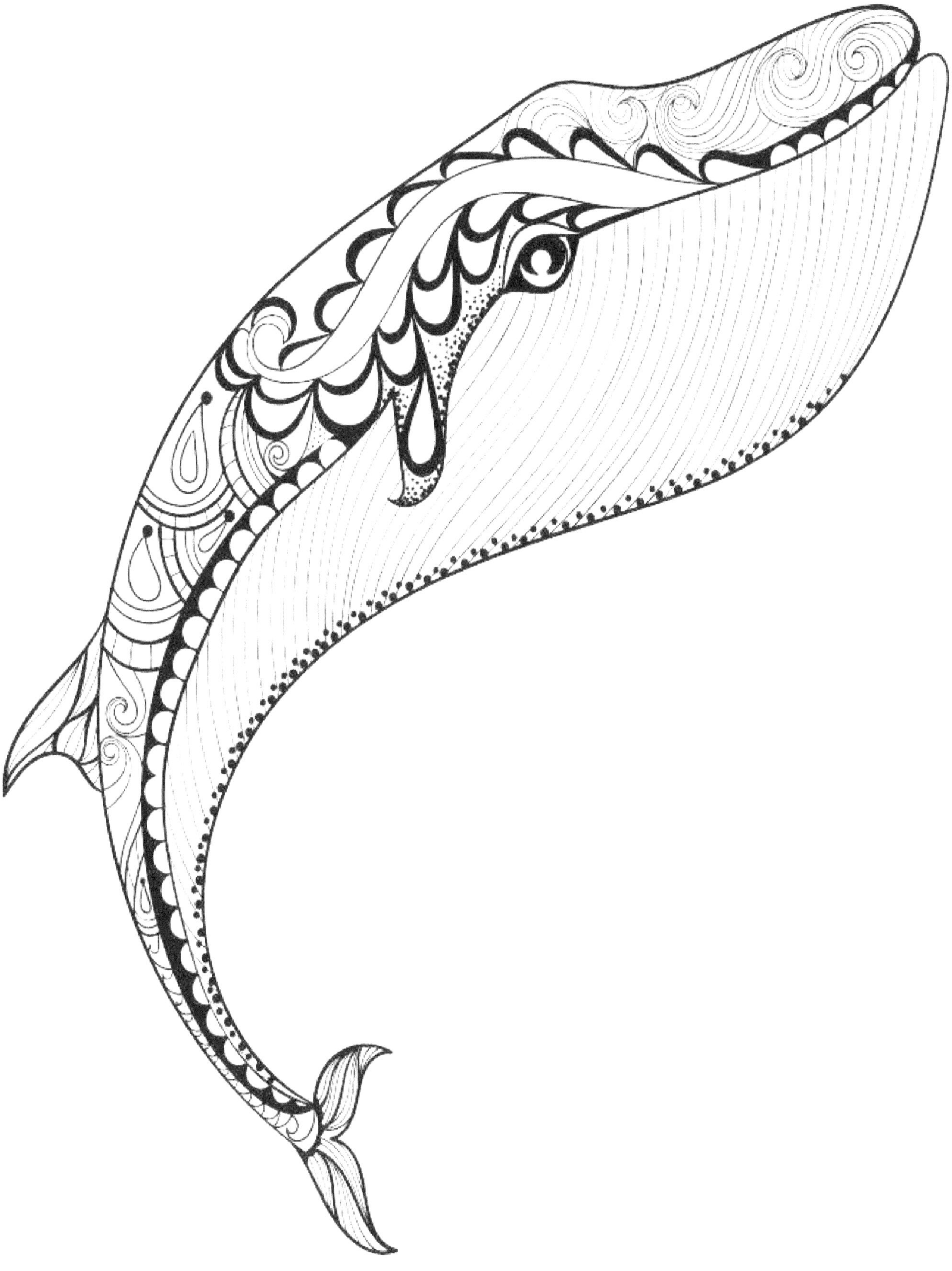

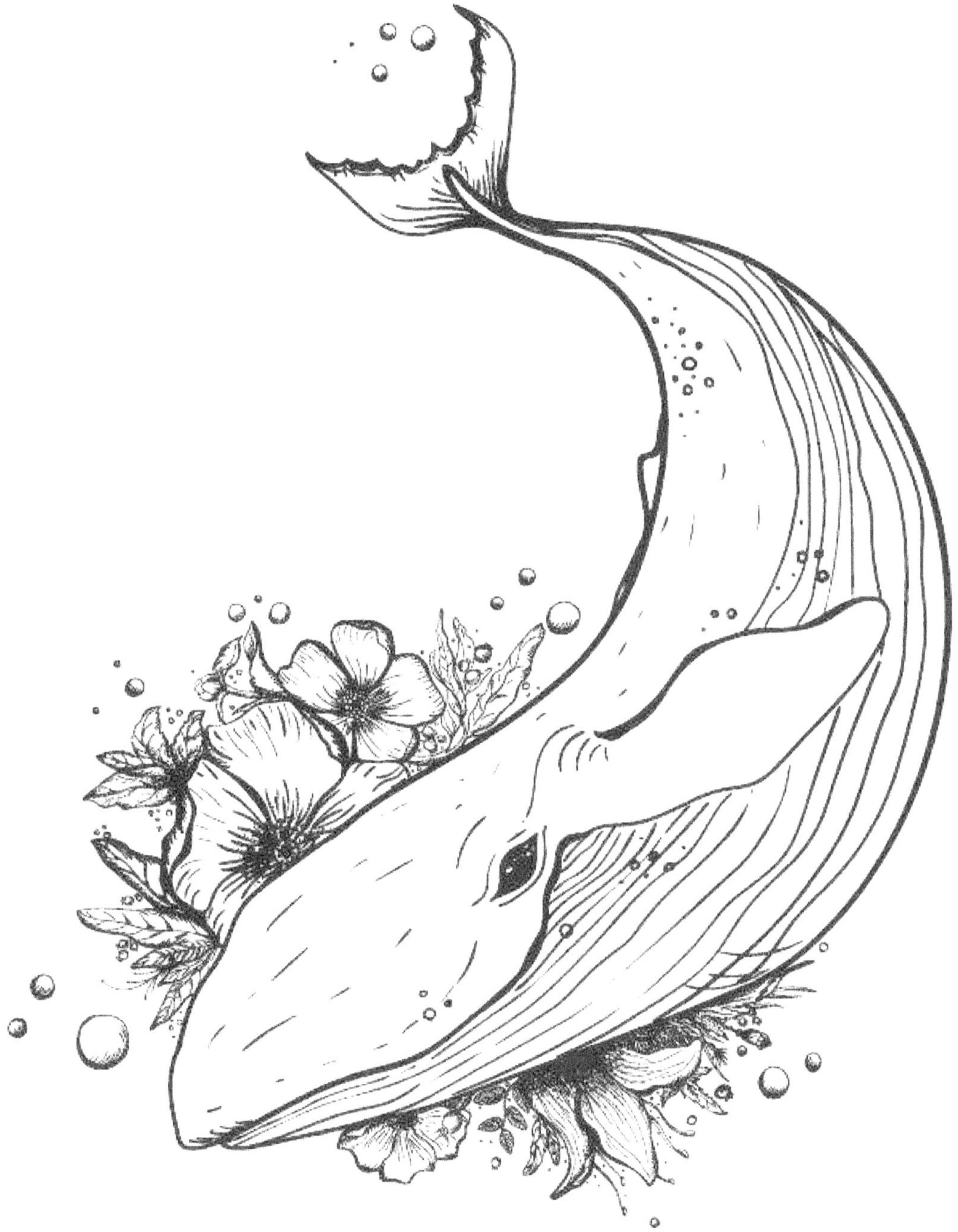

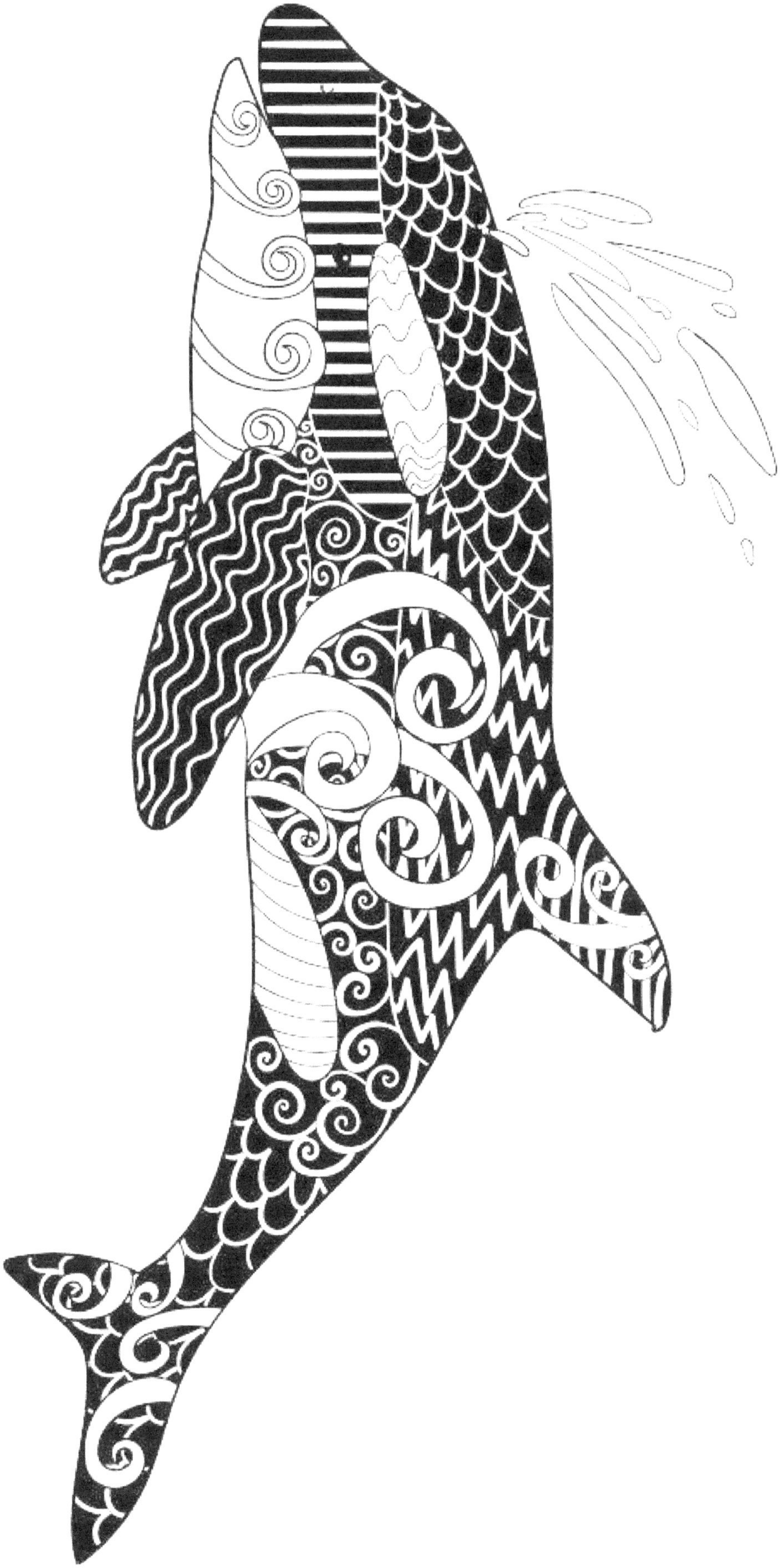

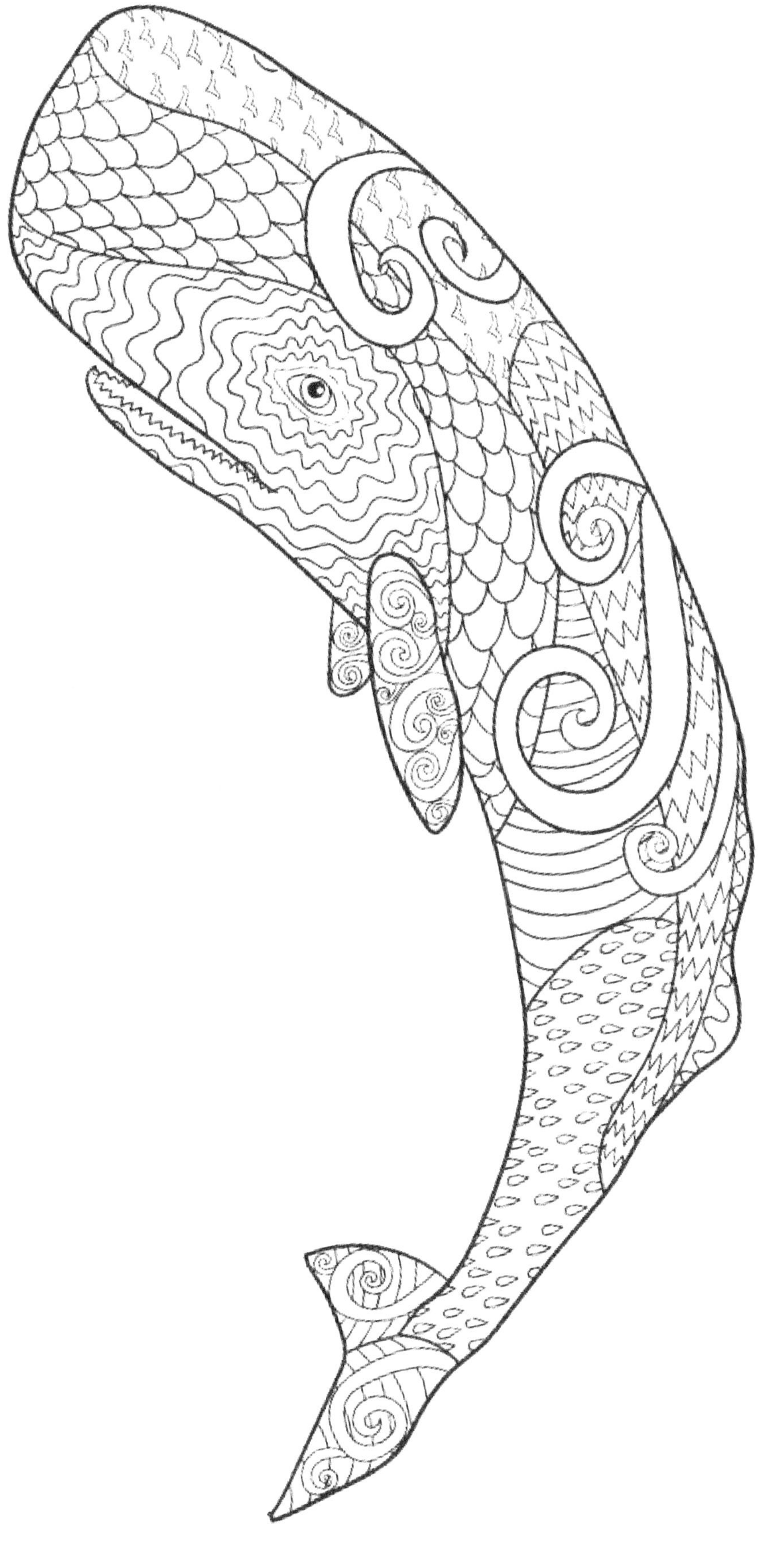

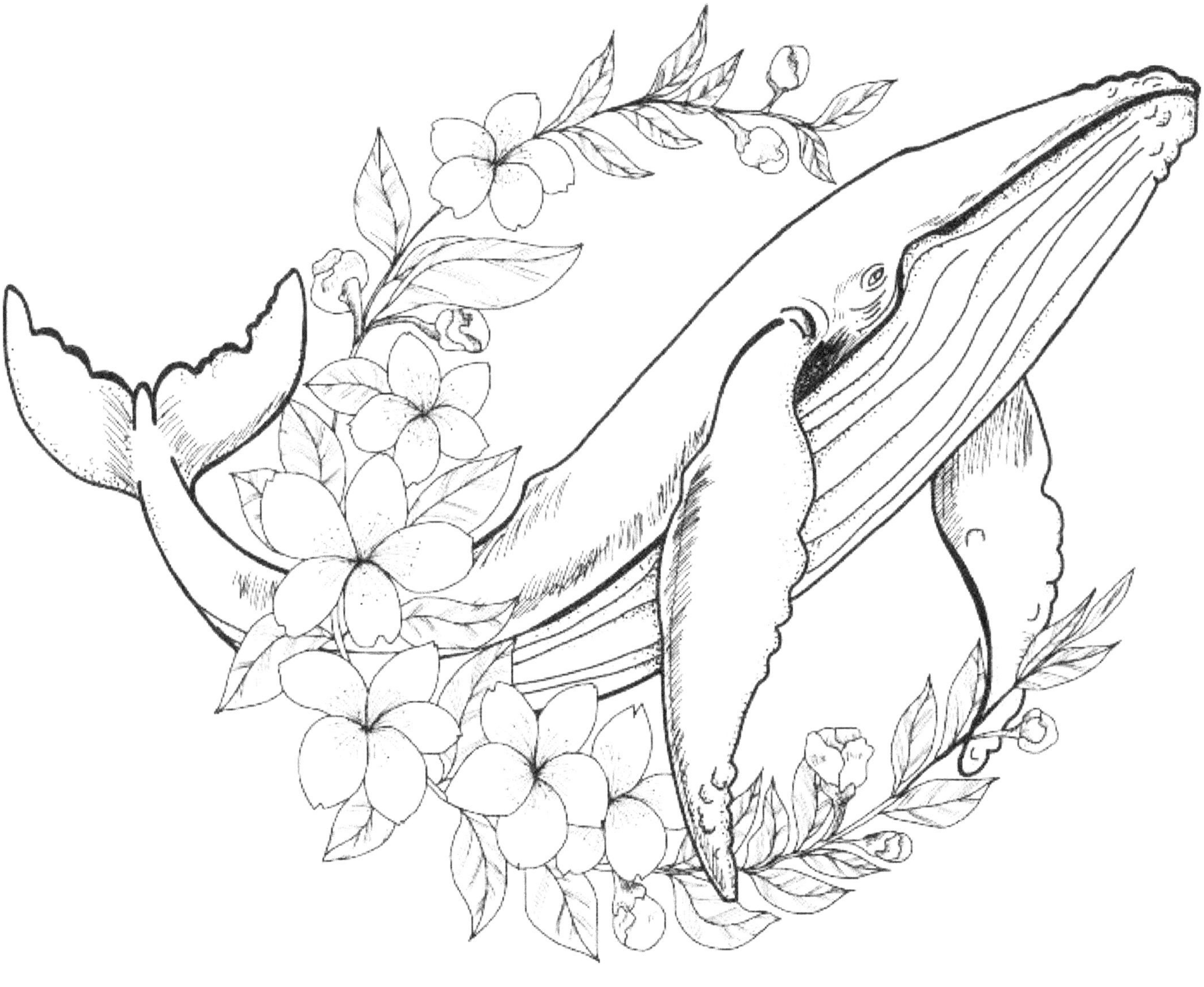

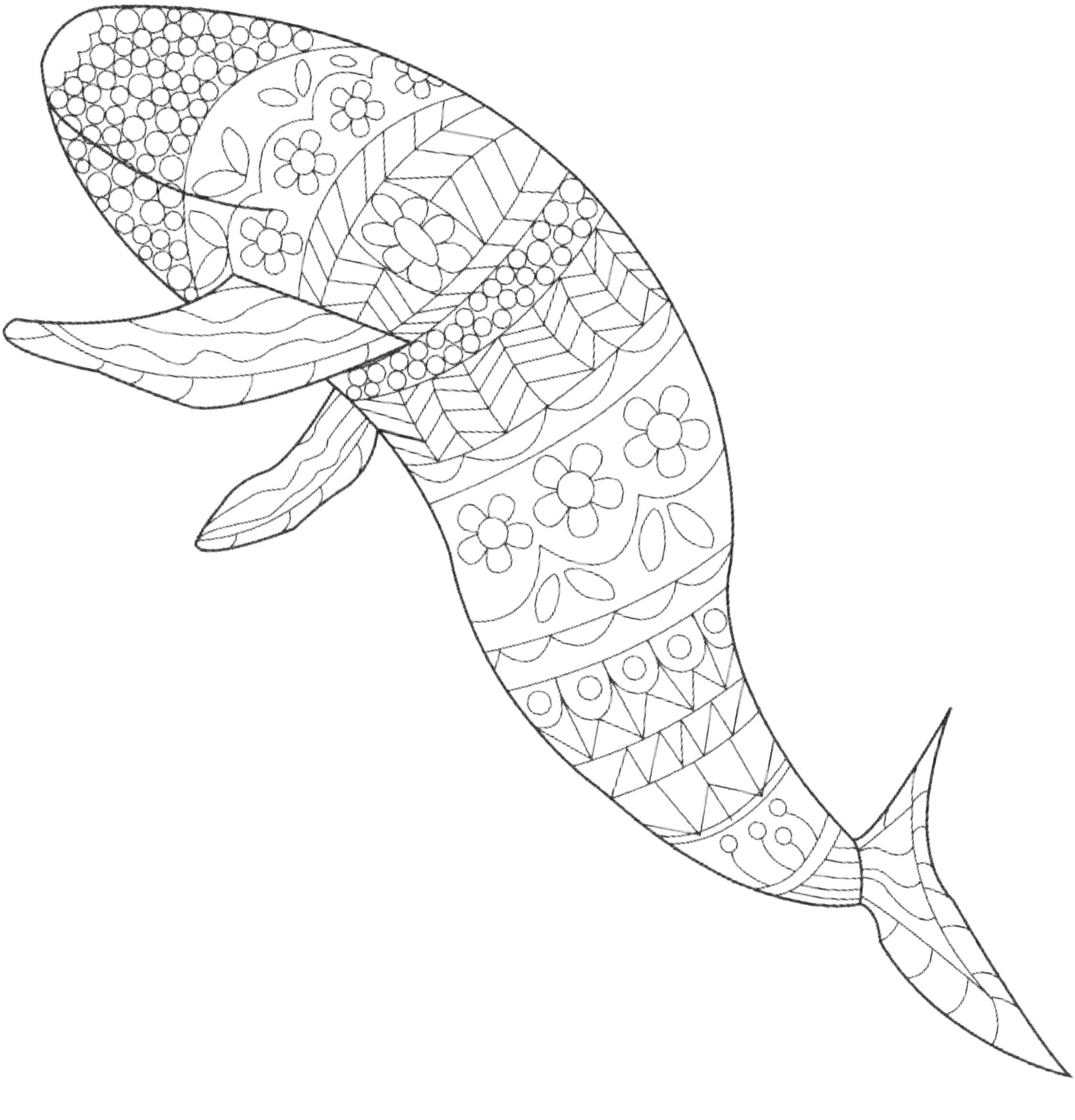

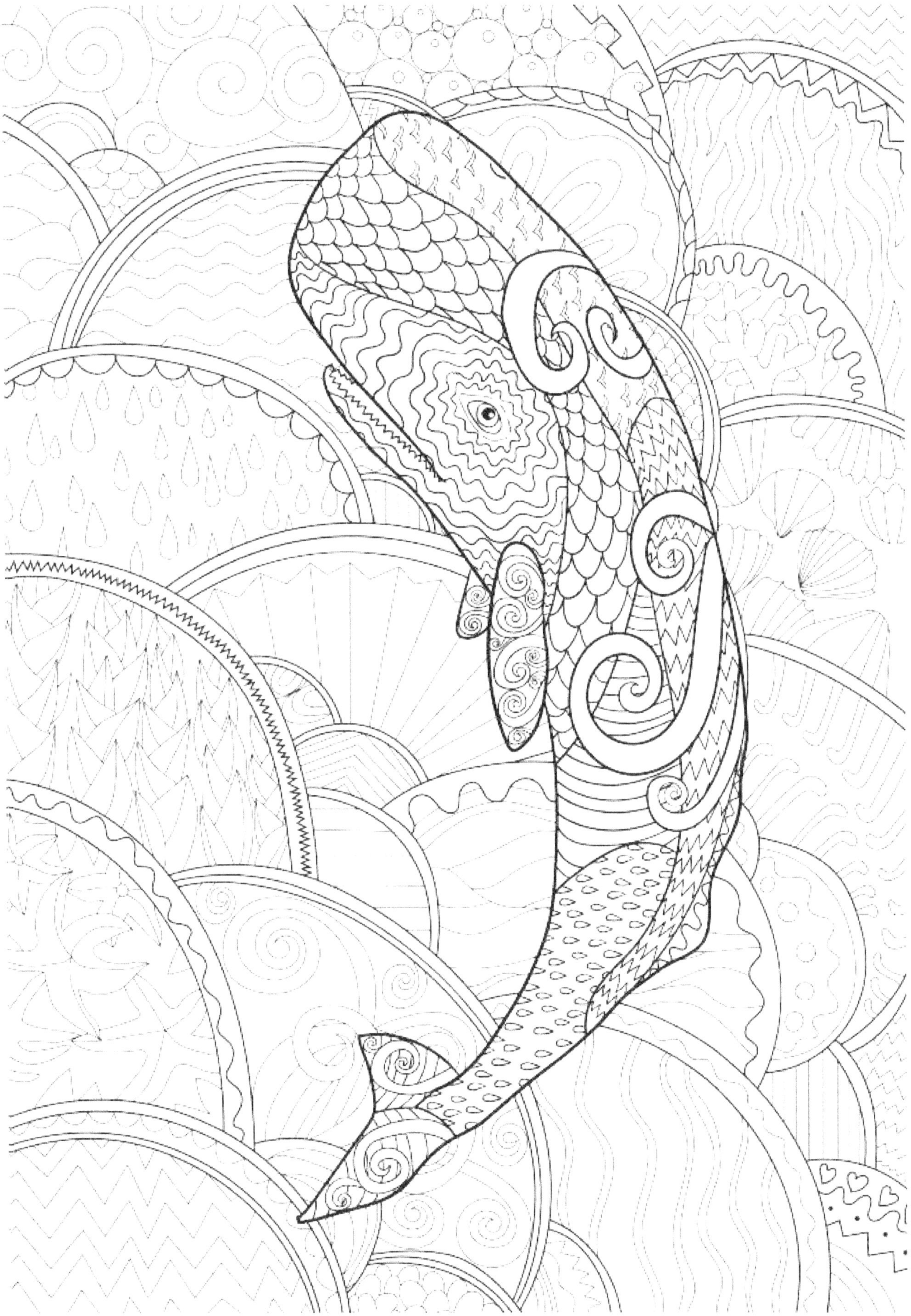

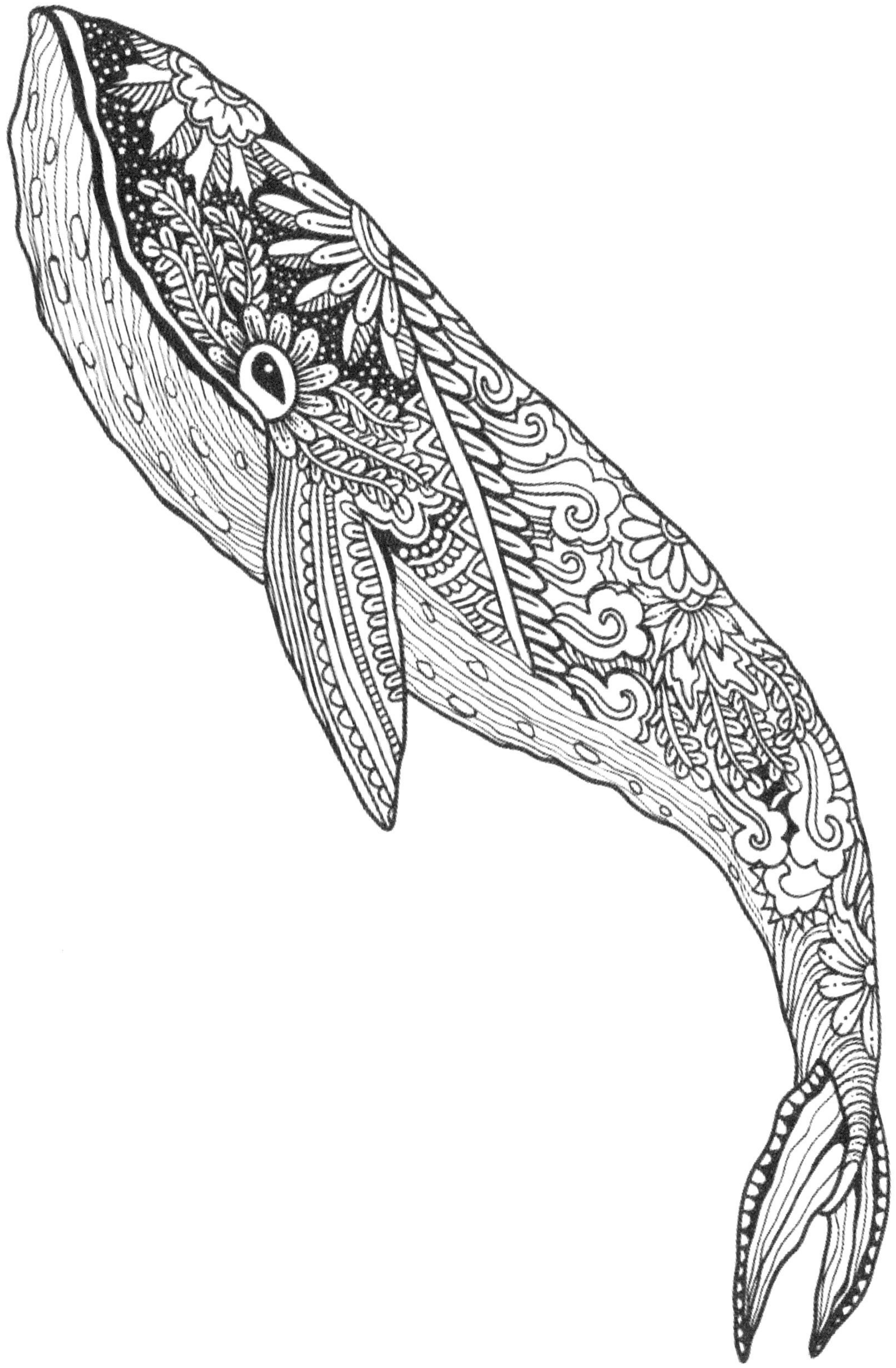

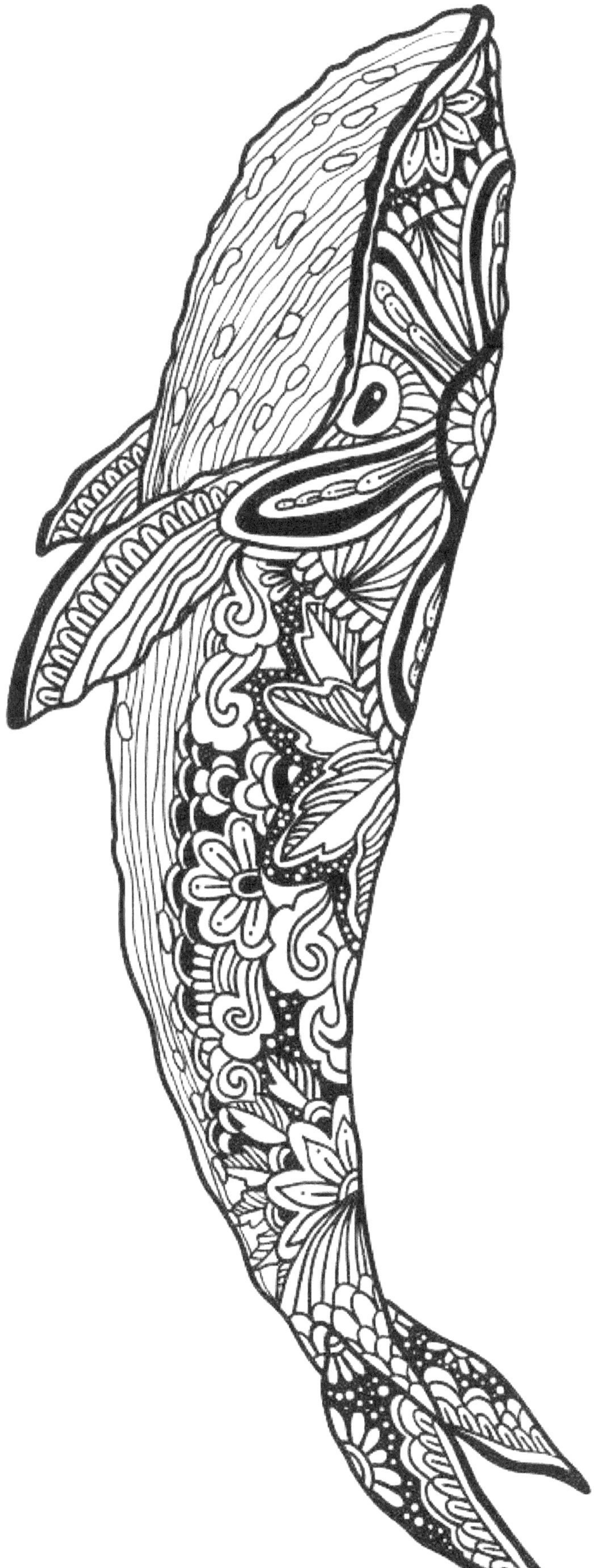

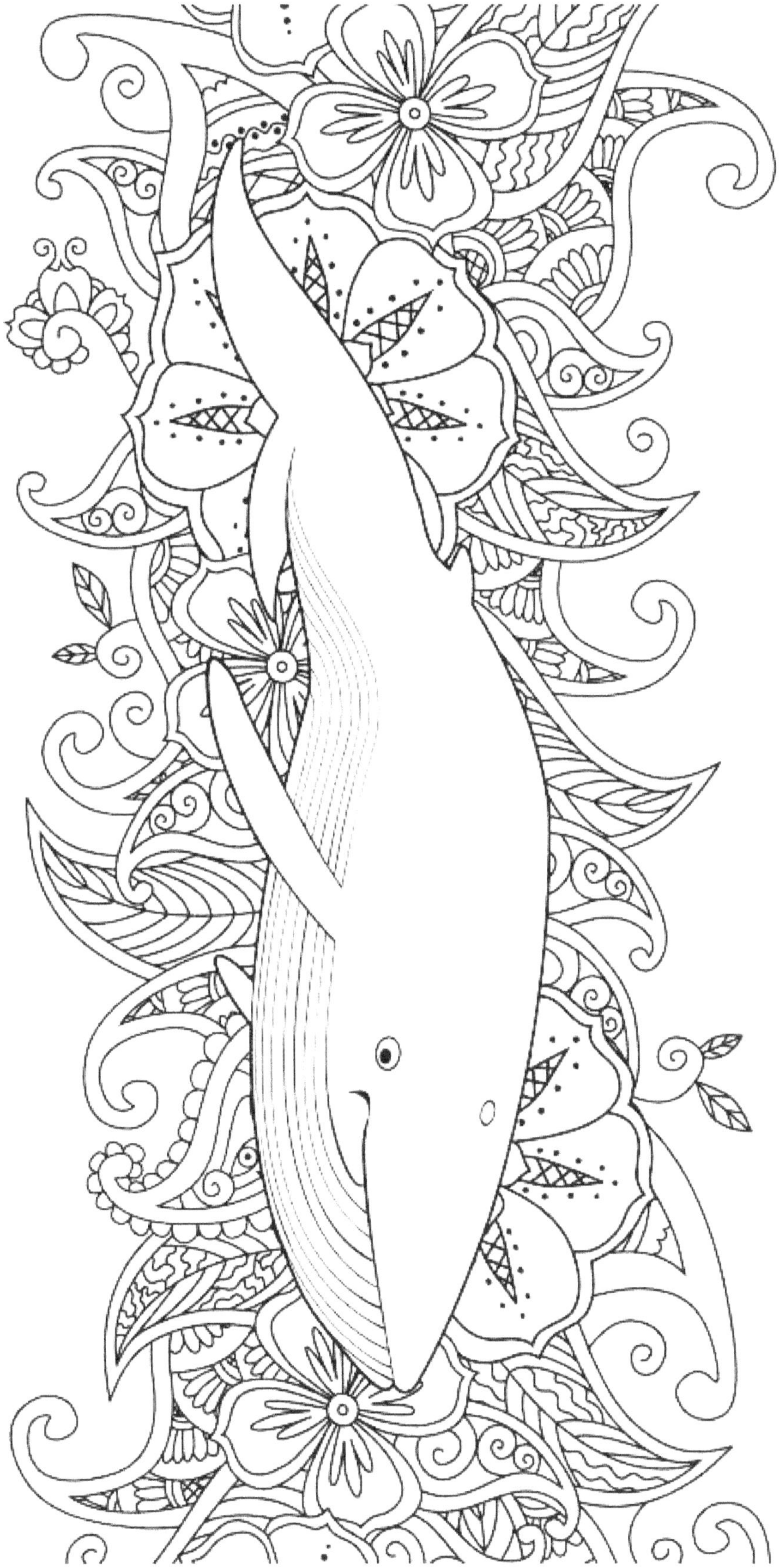

Free Surprise Bonus of Our Horses, Hedgehogs & Turtles Coloring Book For Adults. Enjoy!

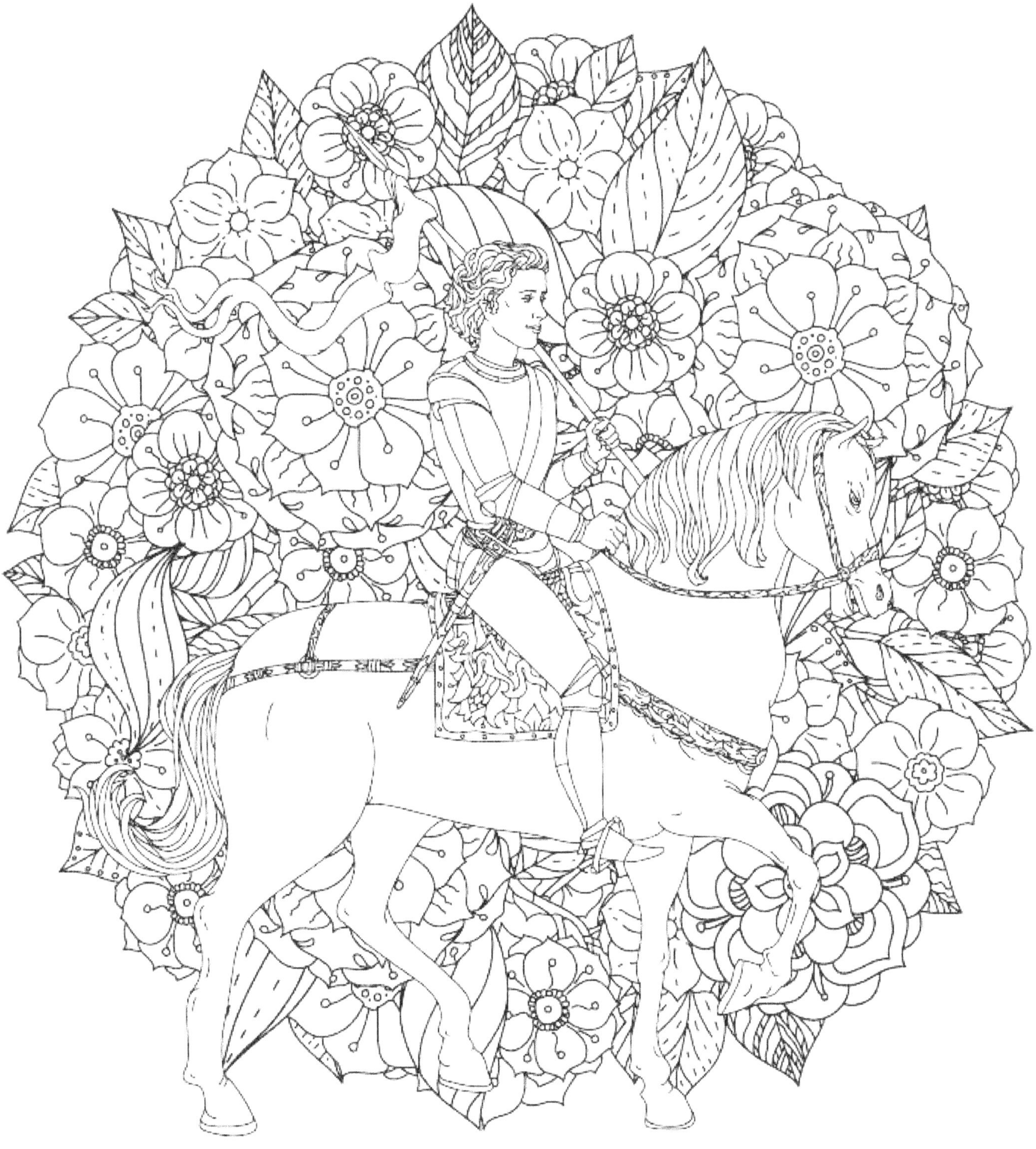

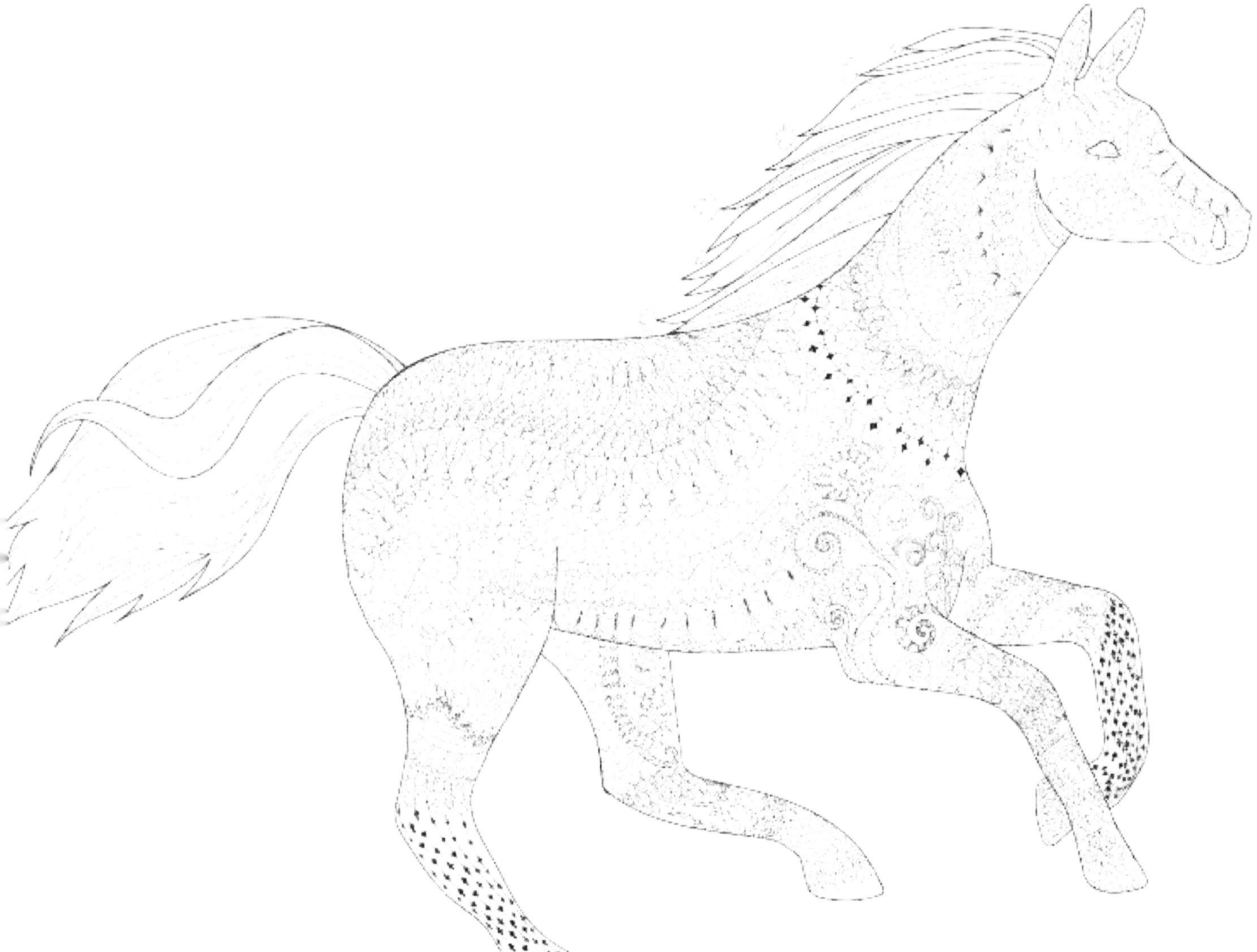

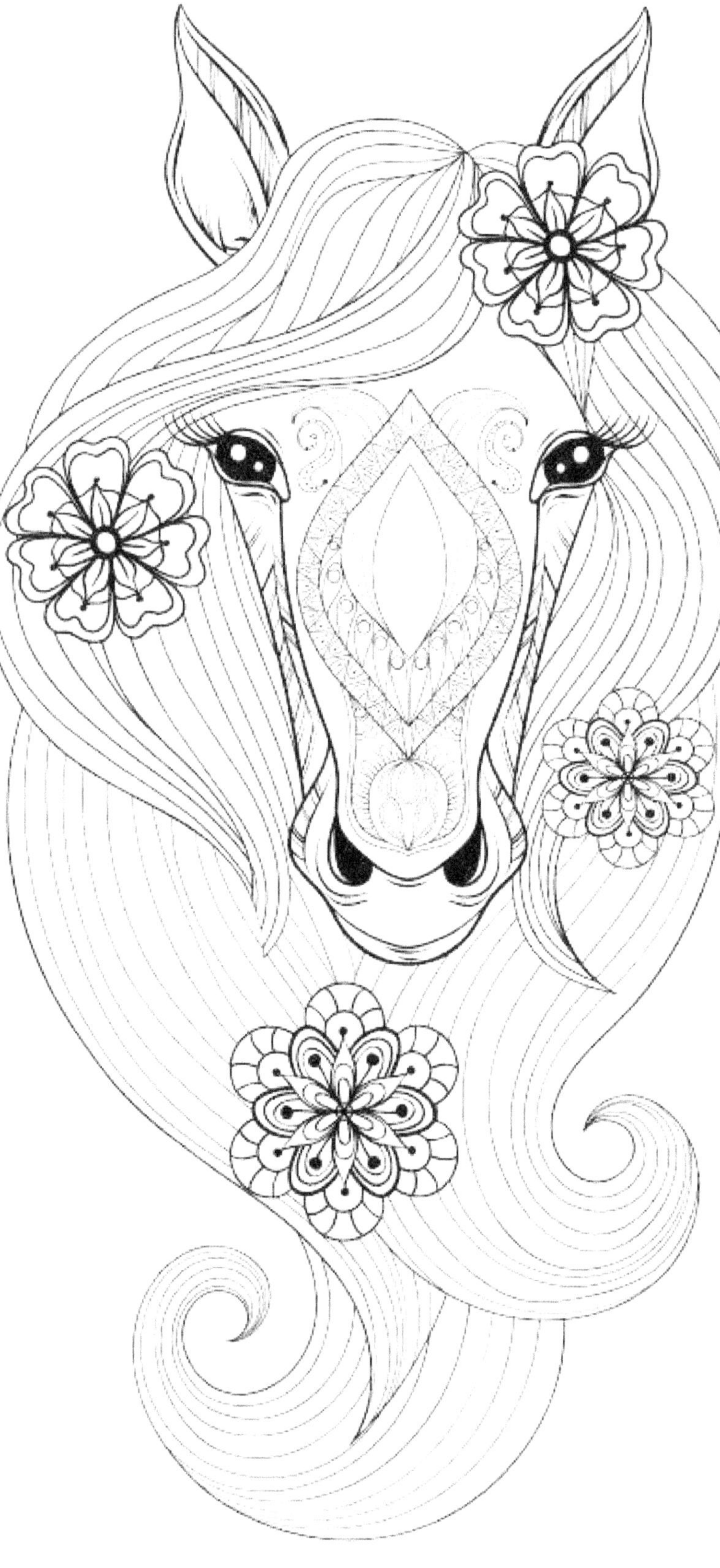

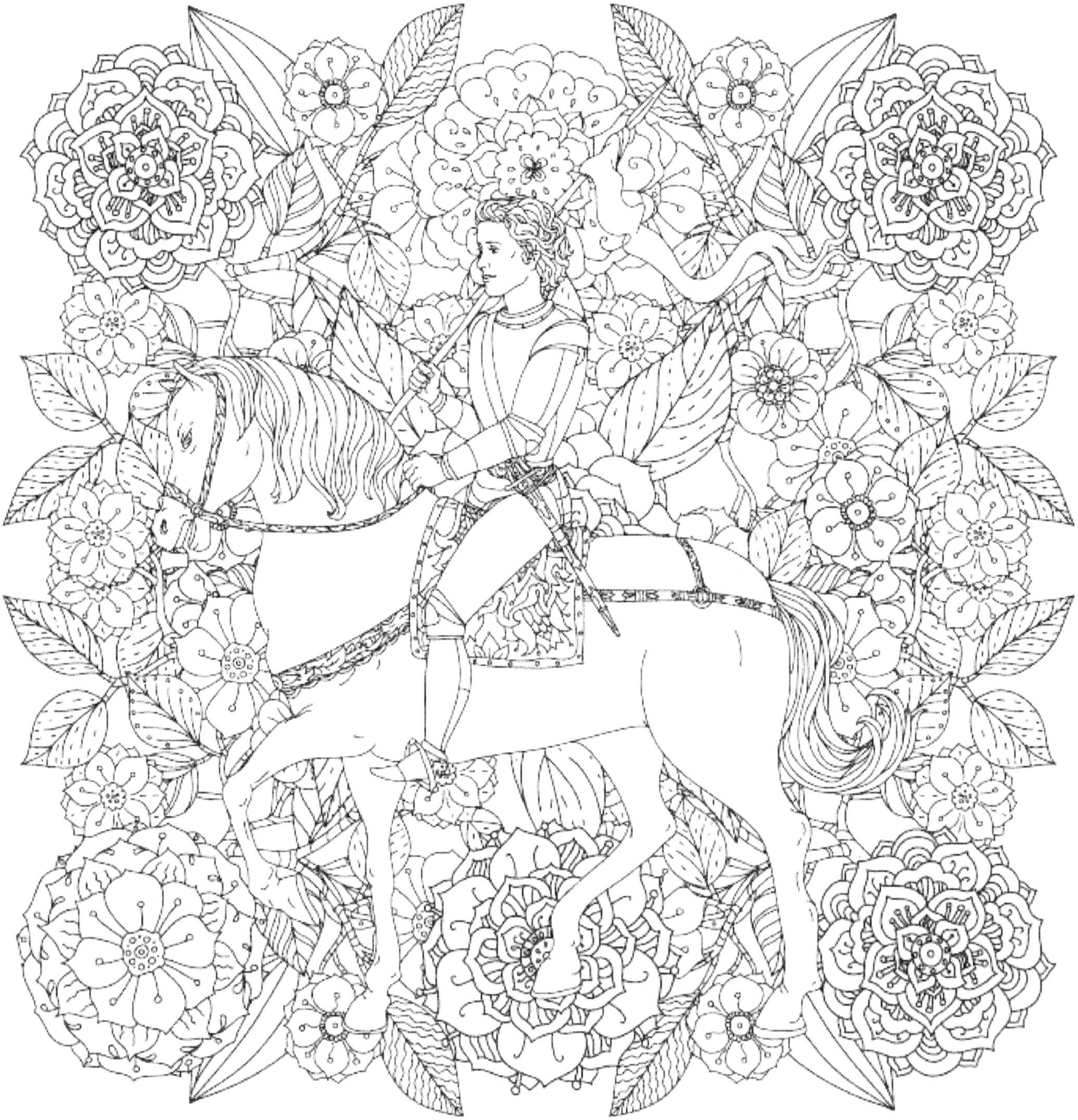

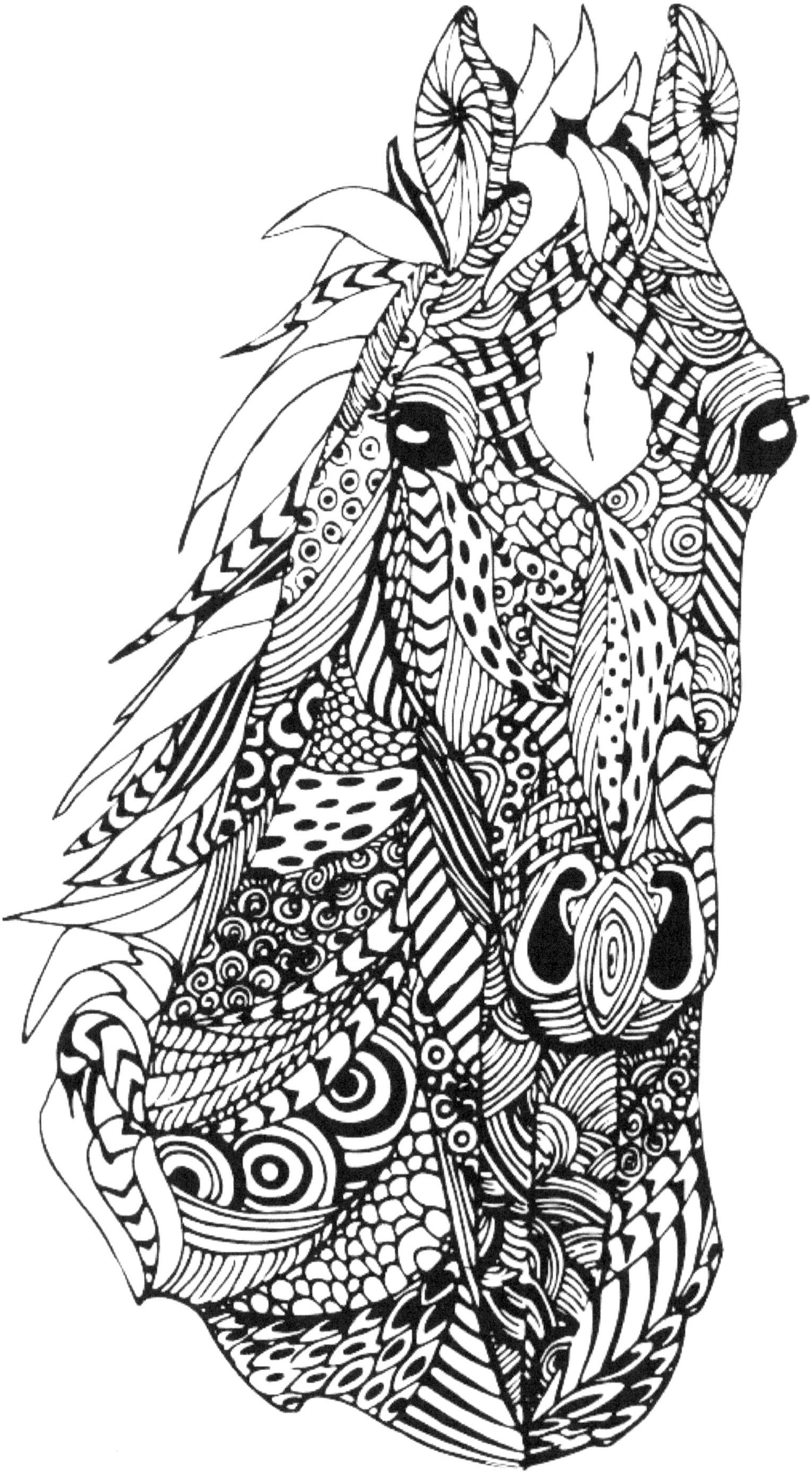

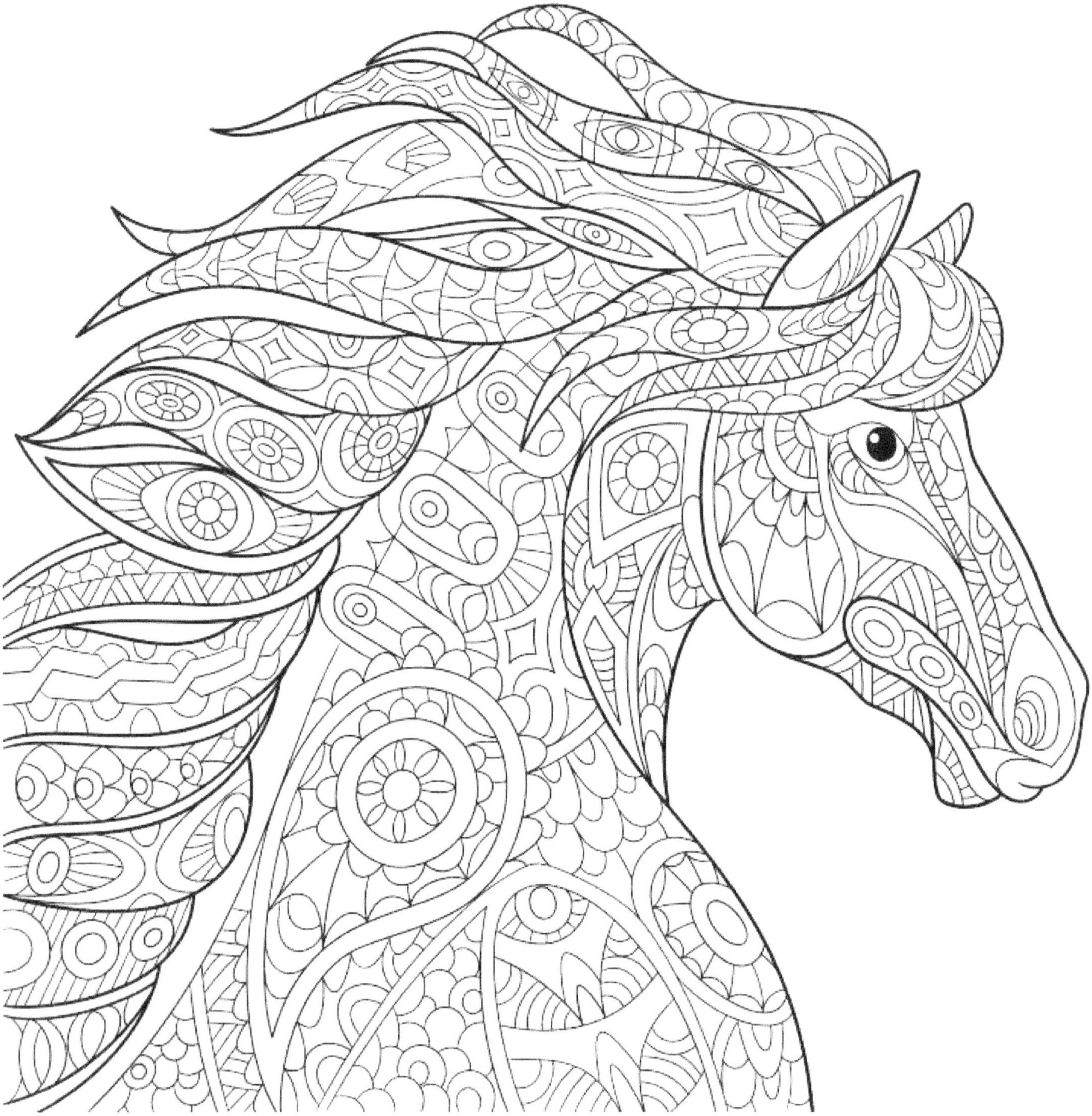

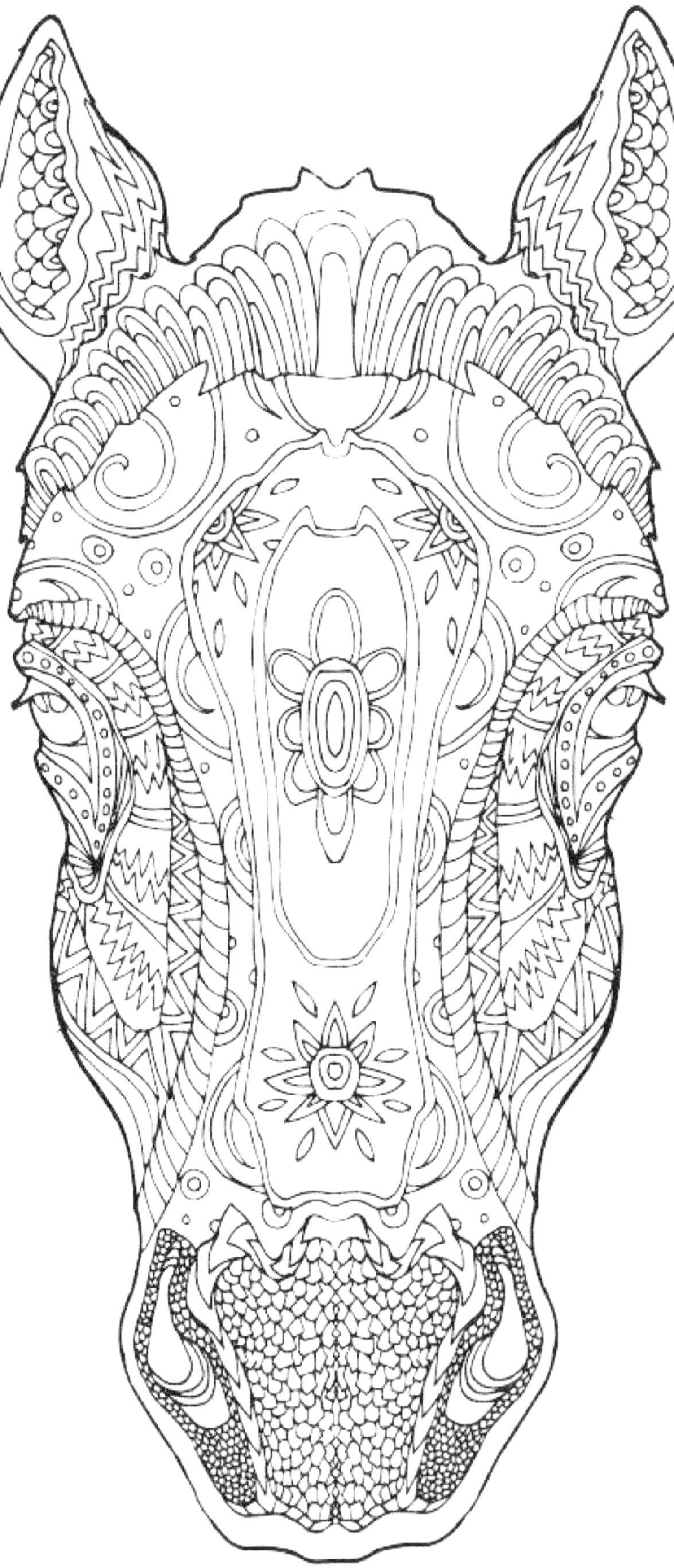

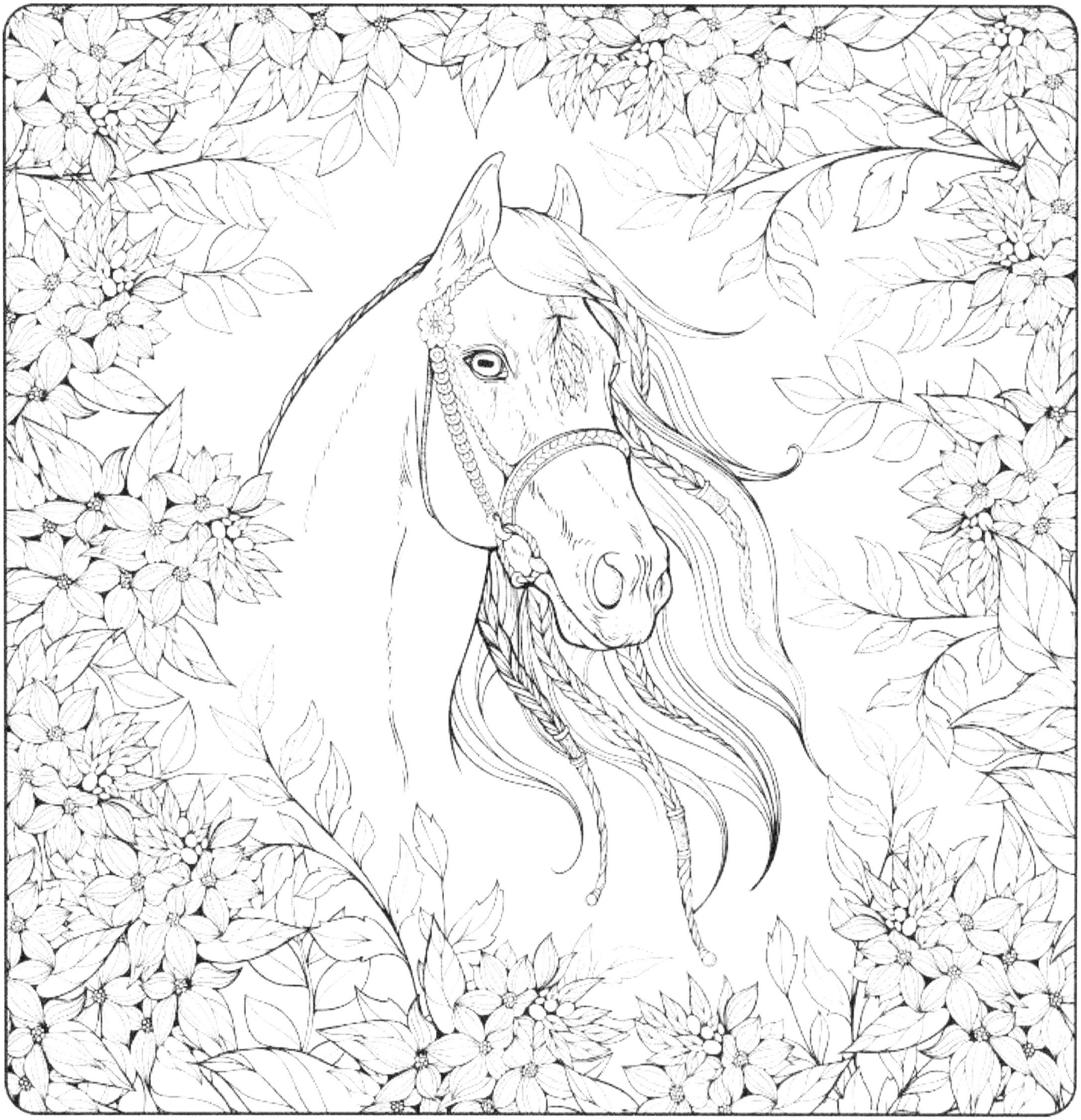

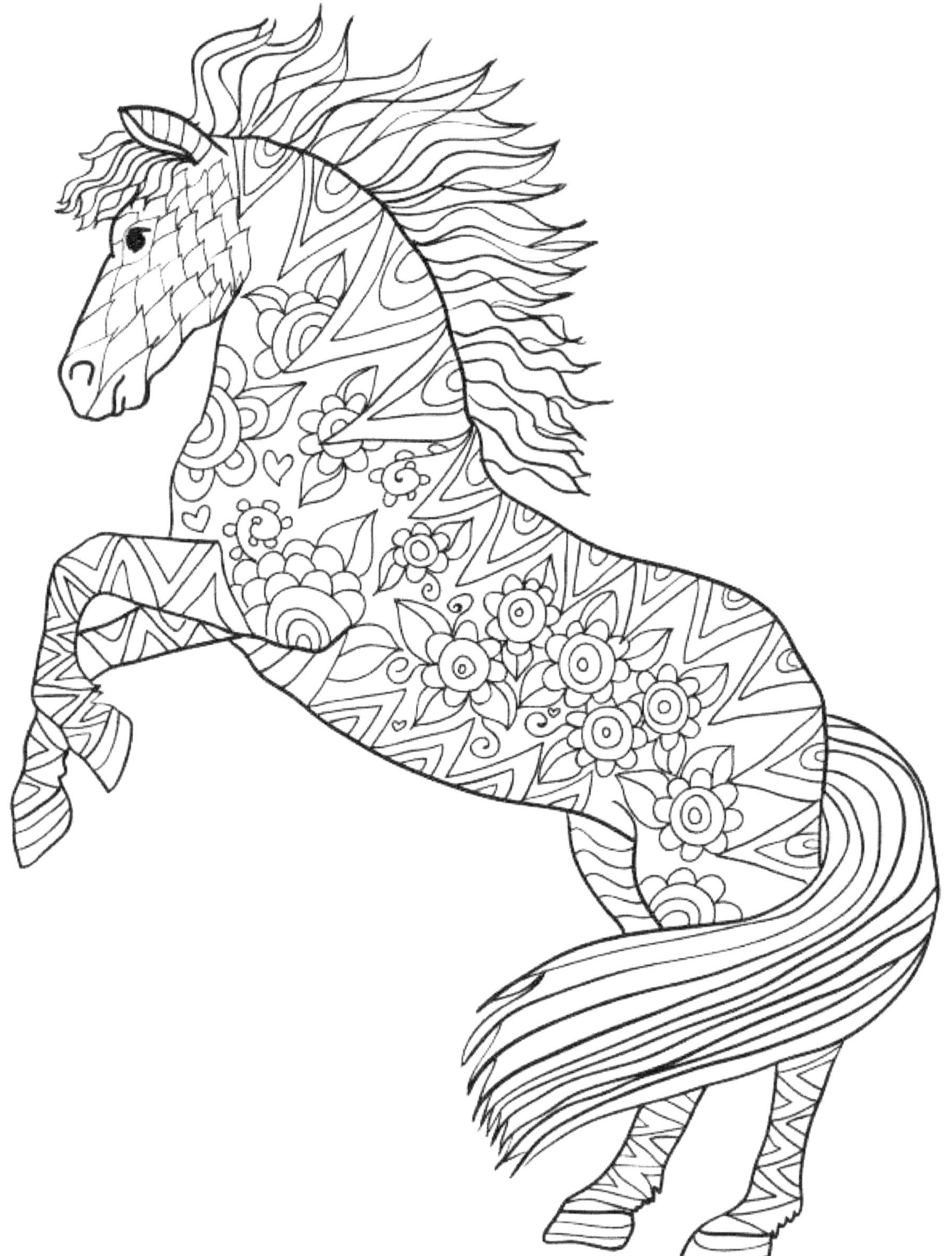

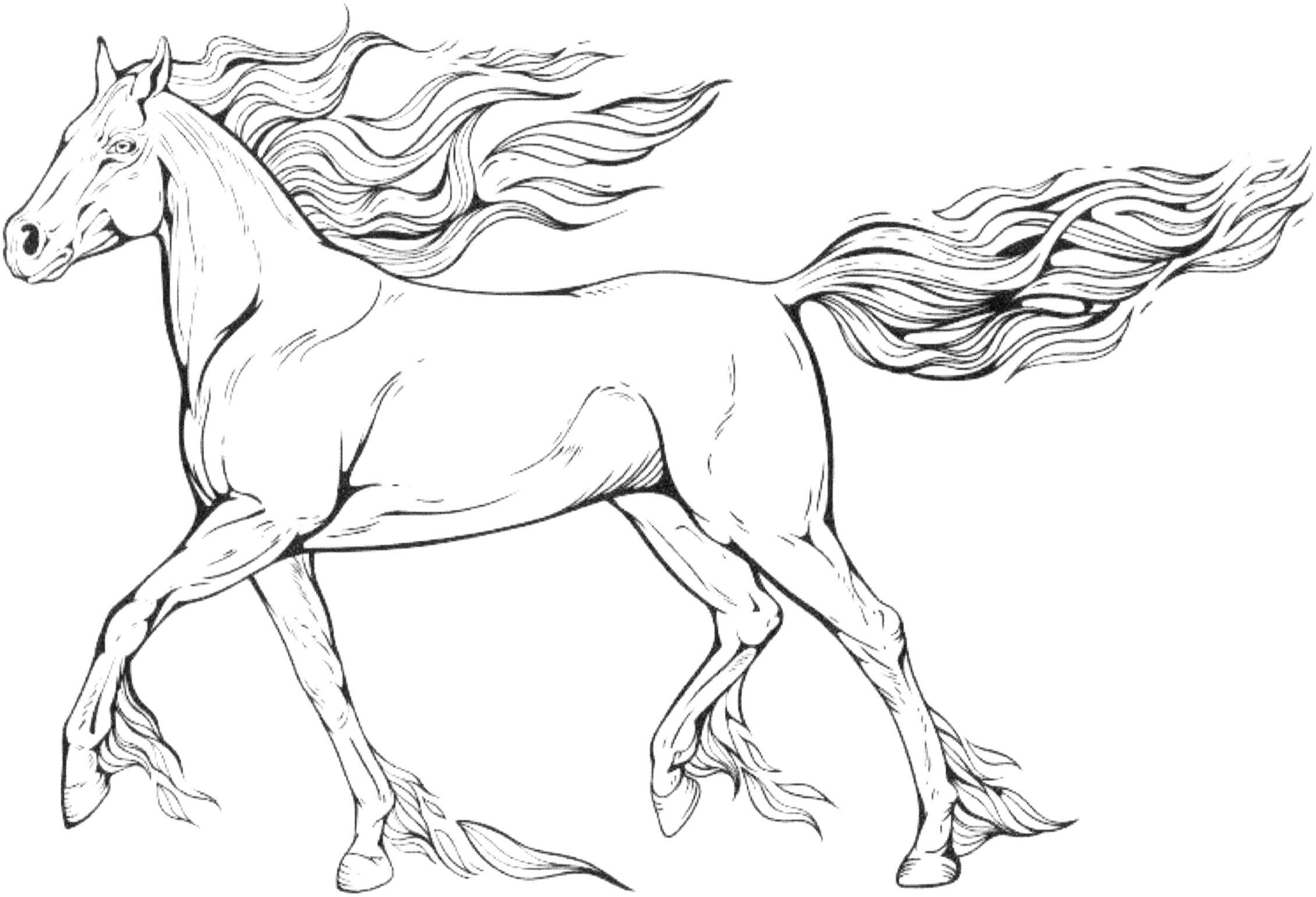

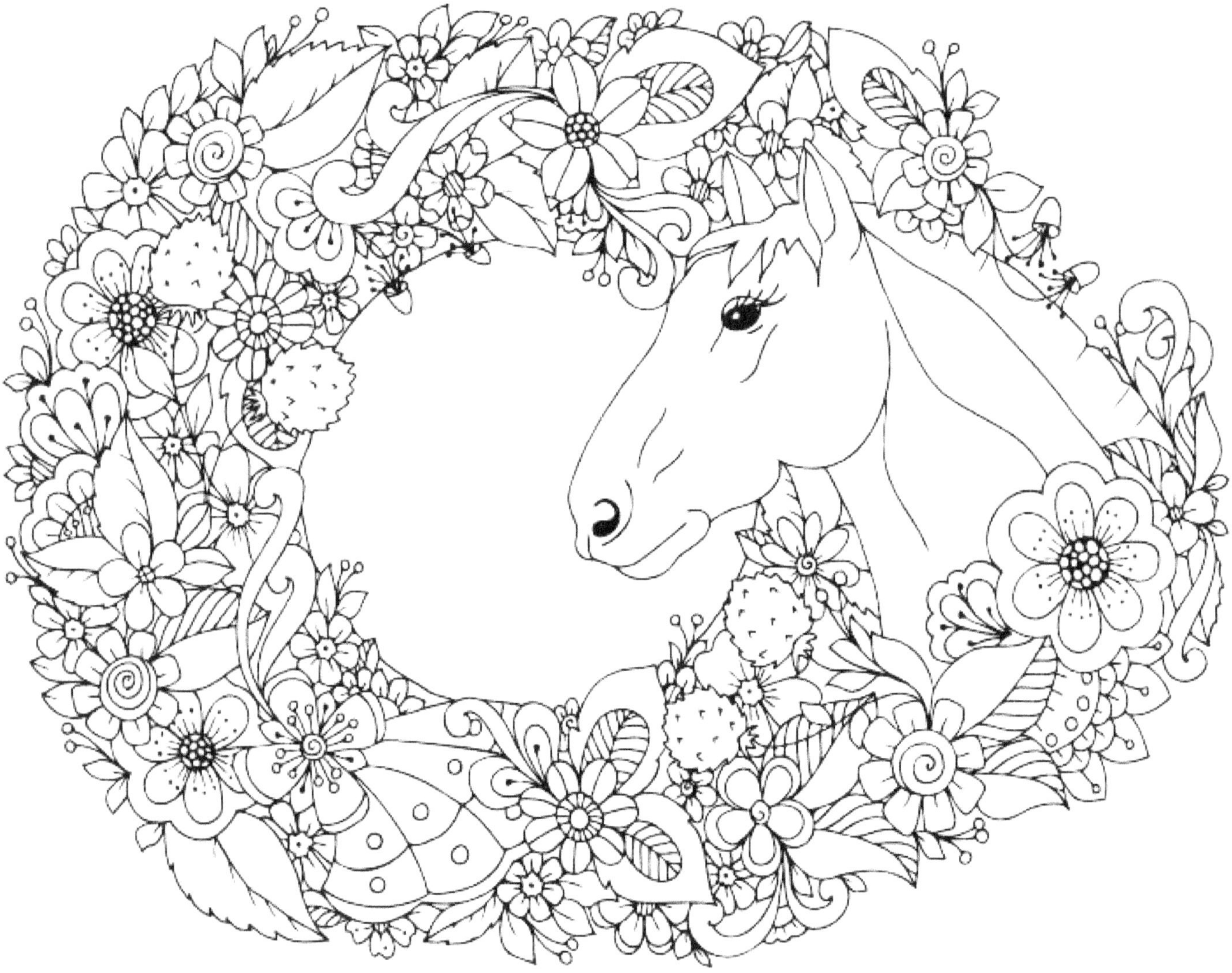

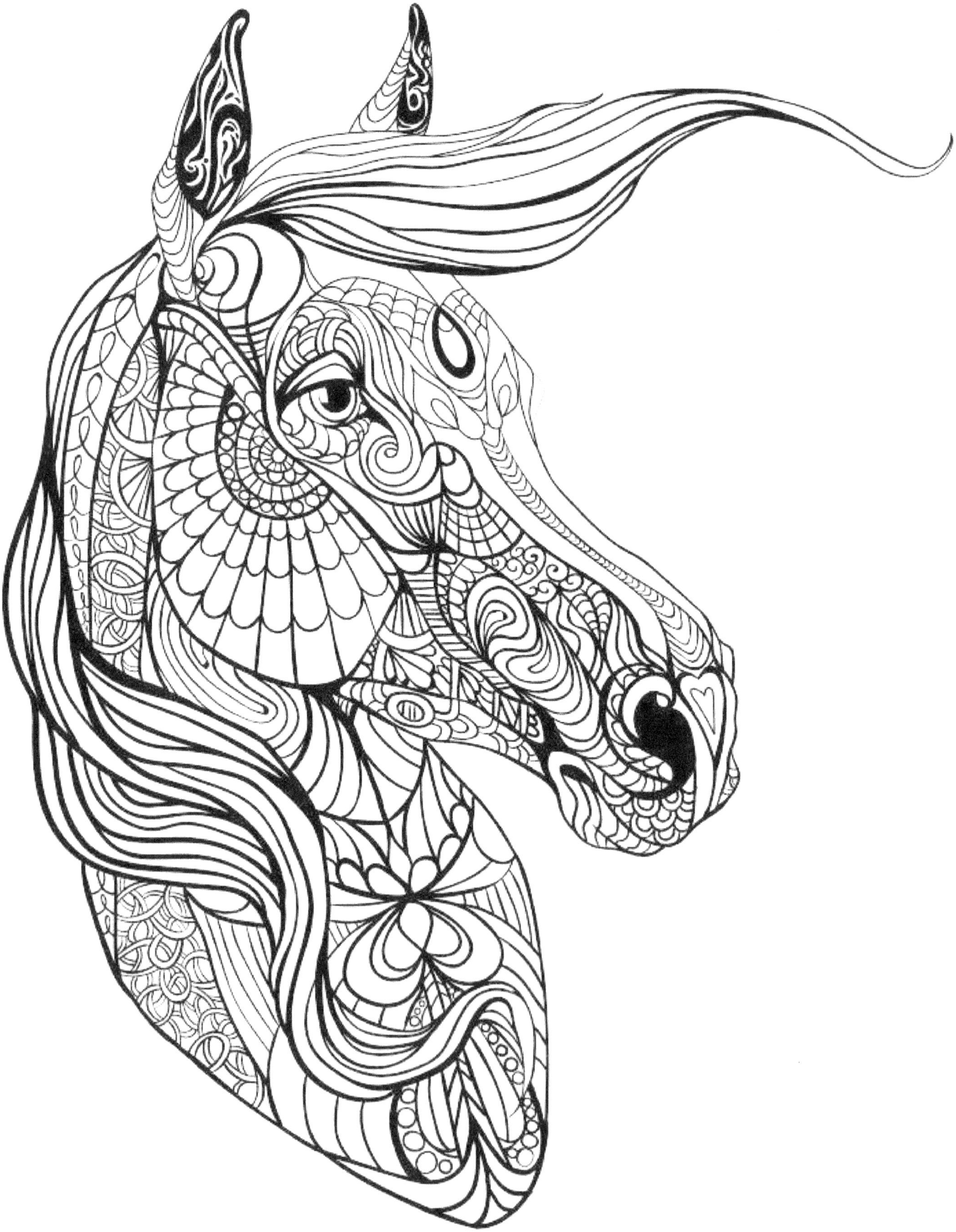

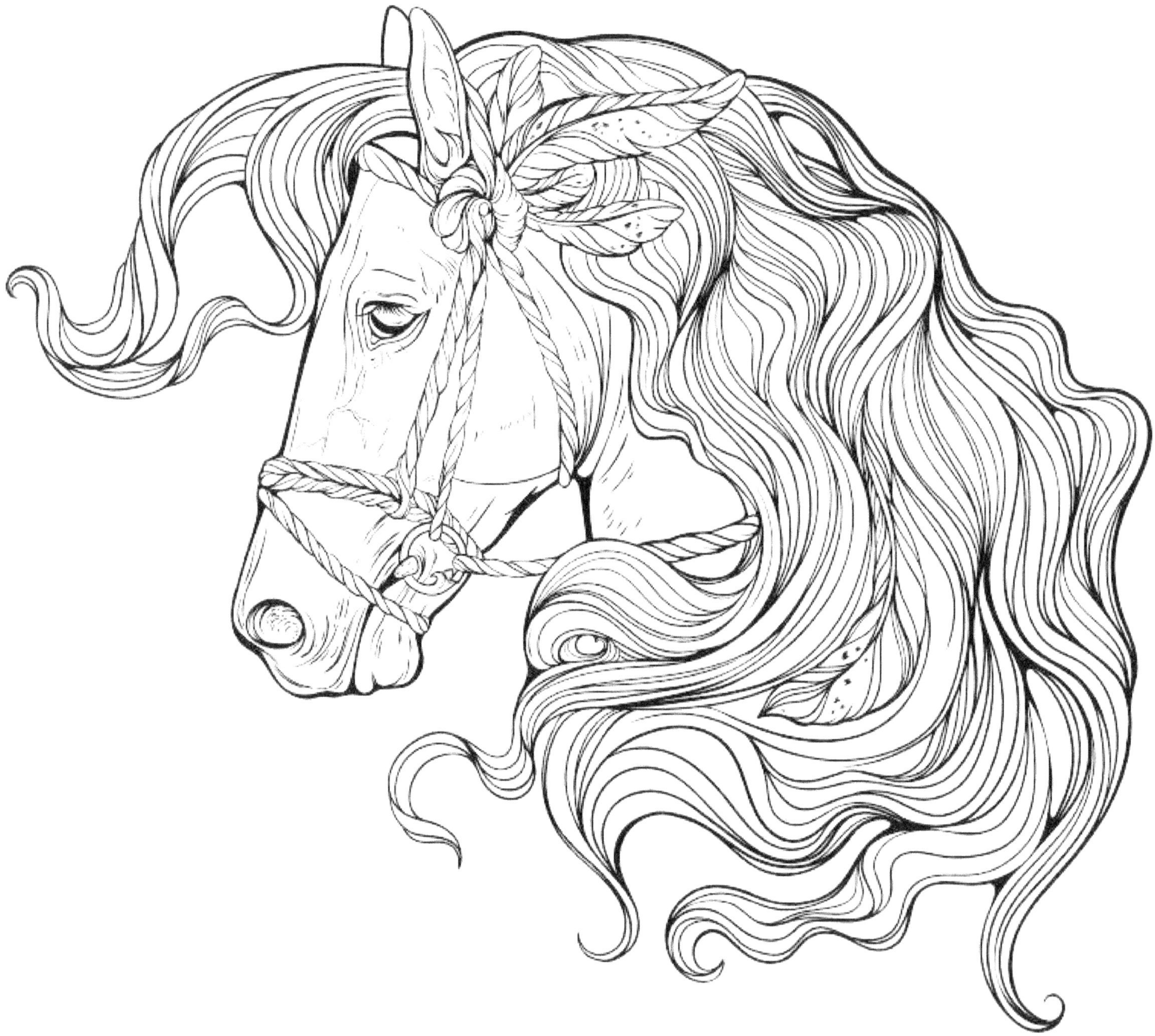

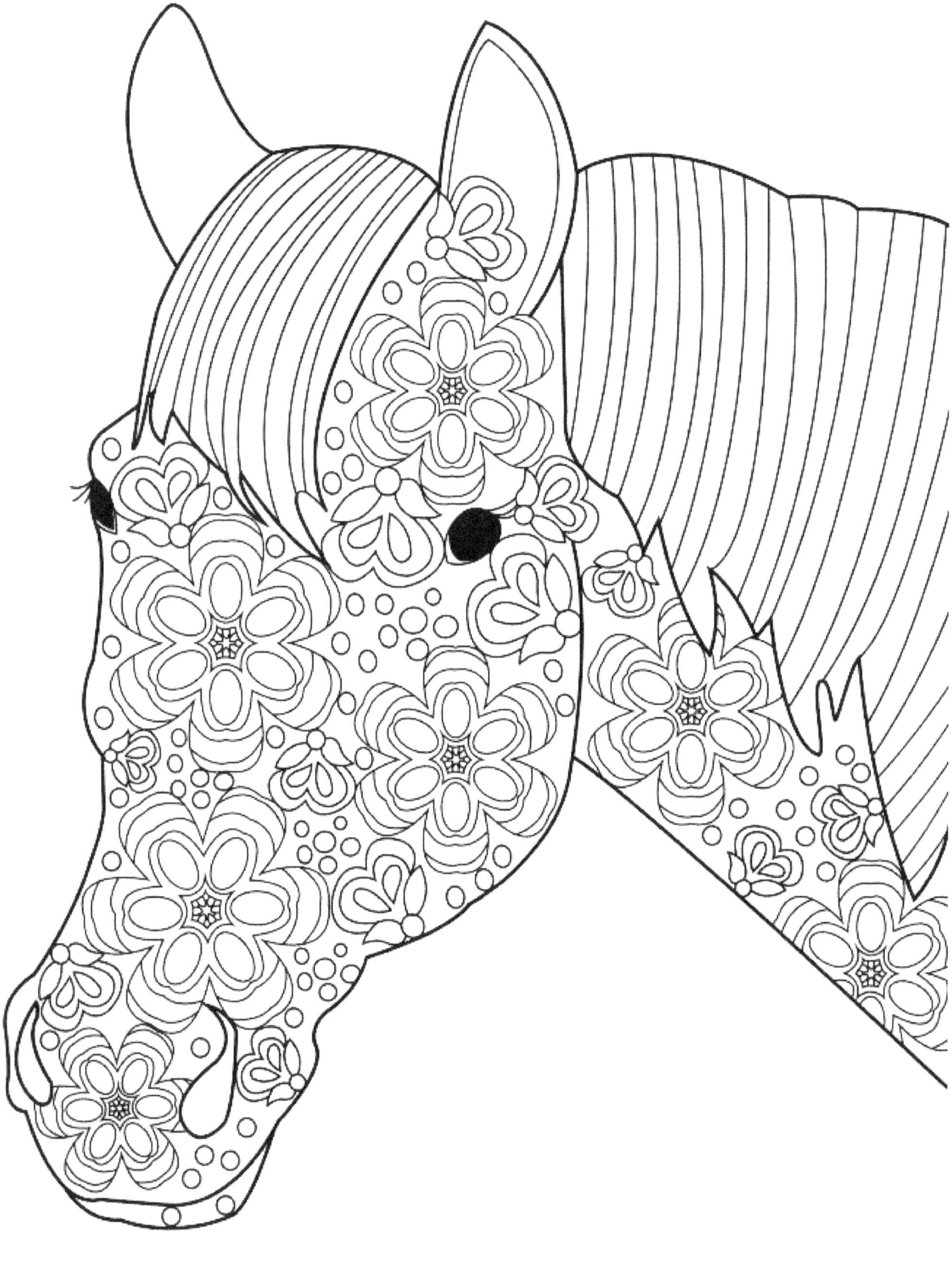

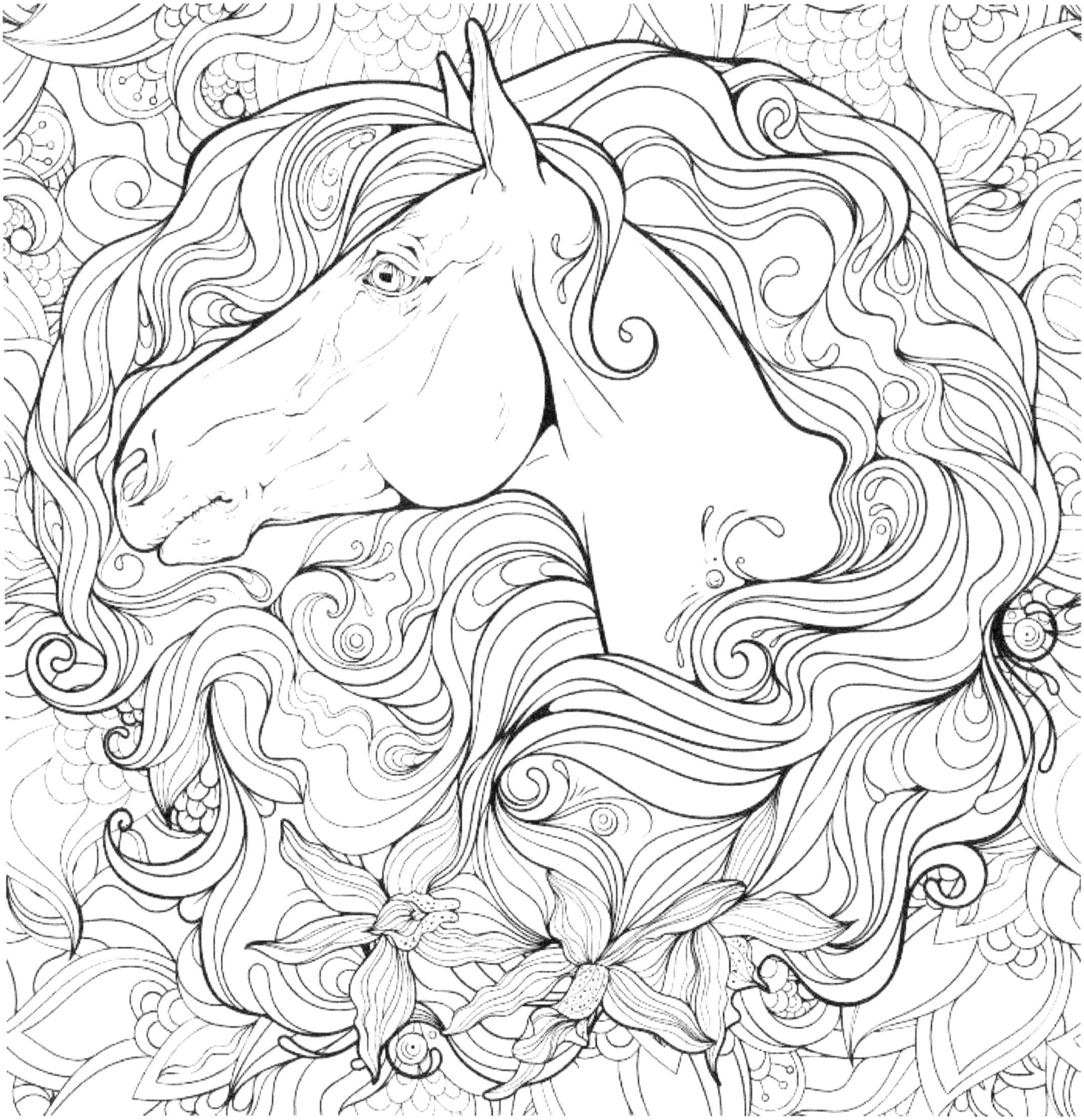

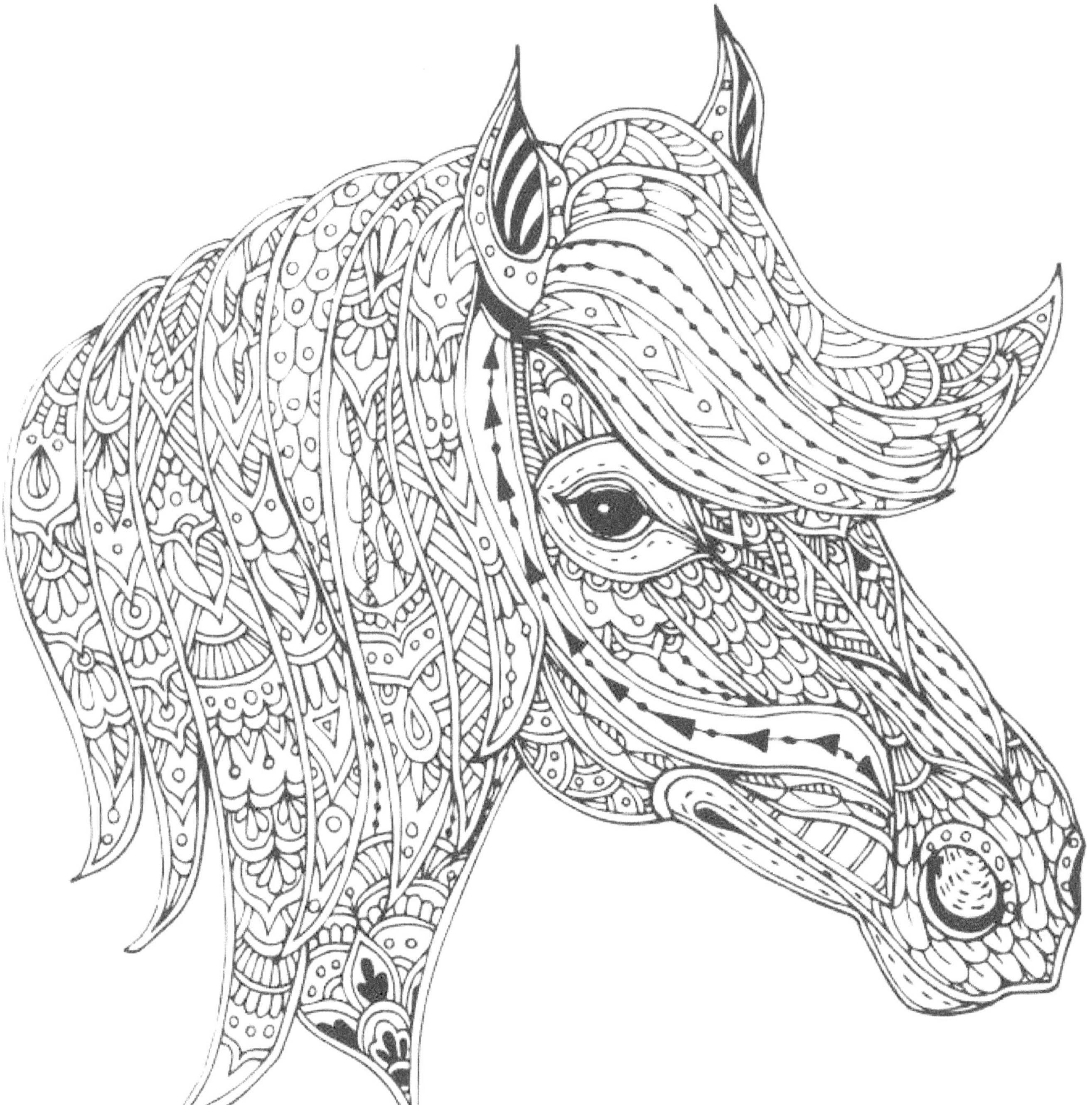

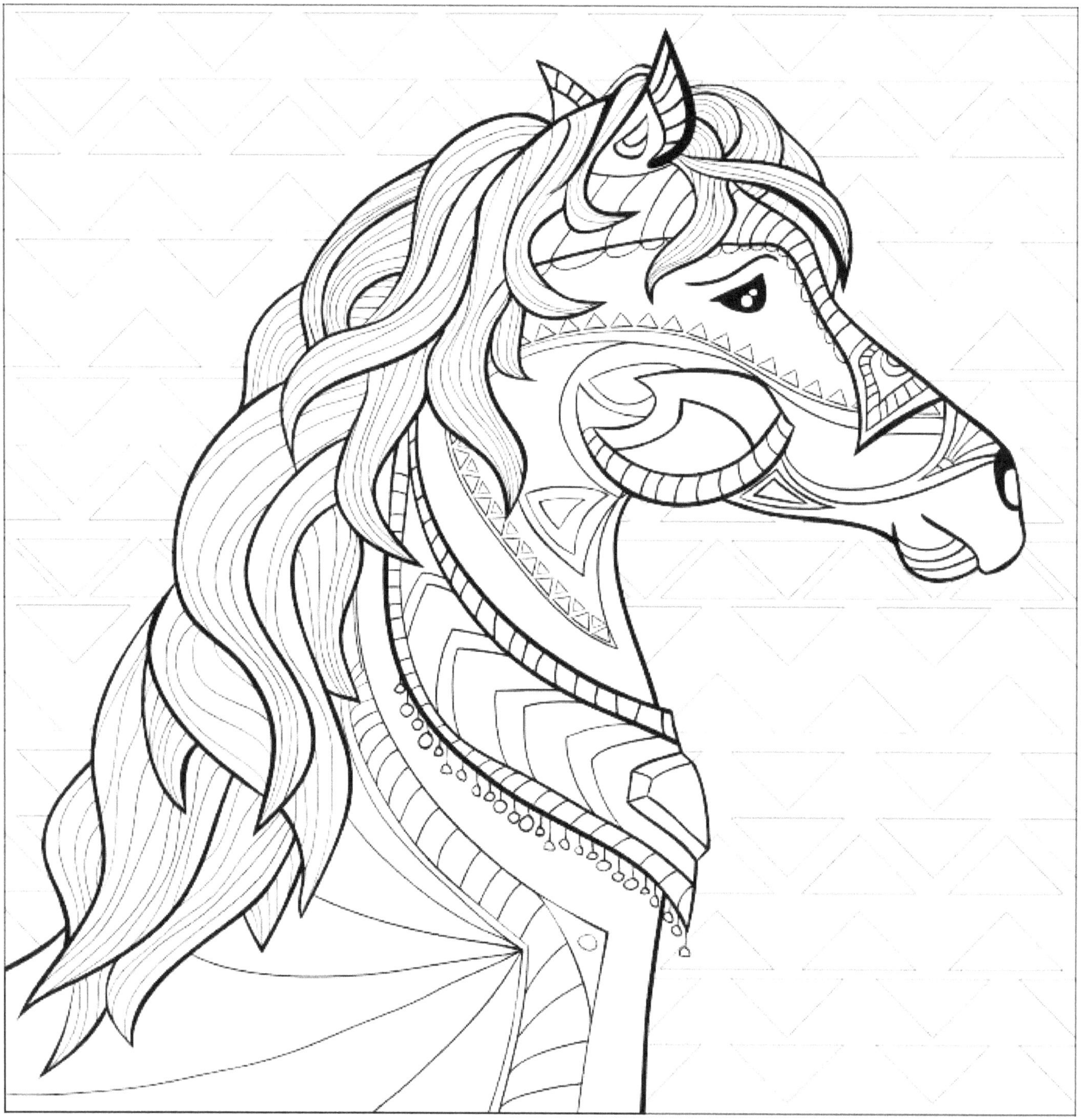

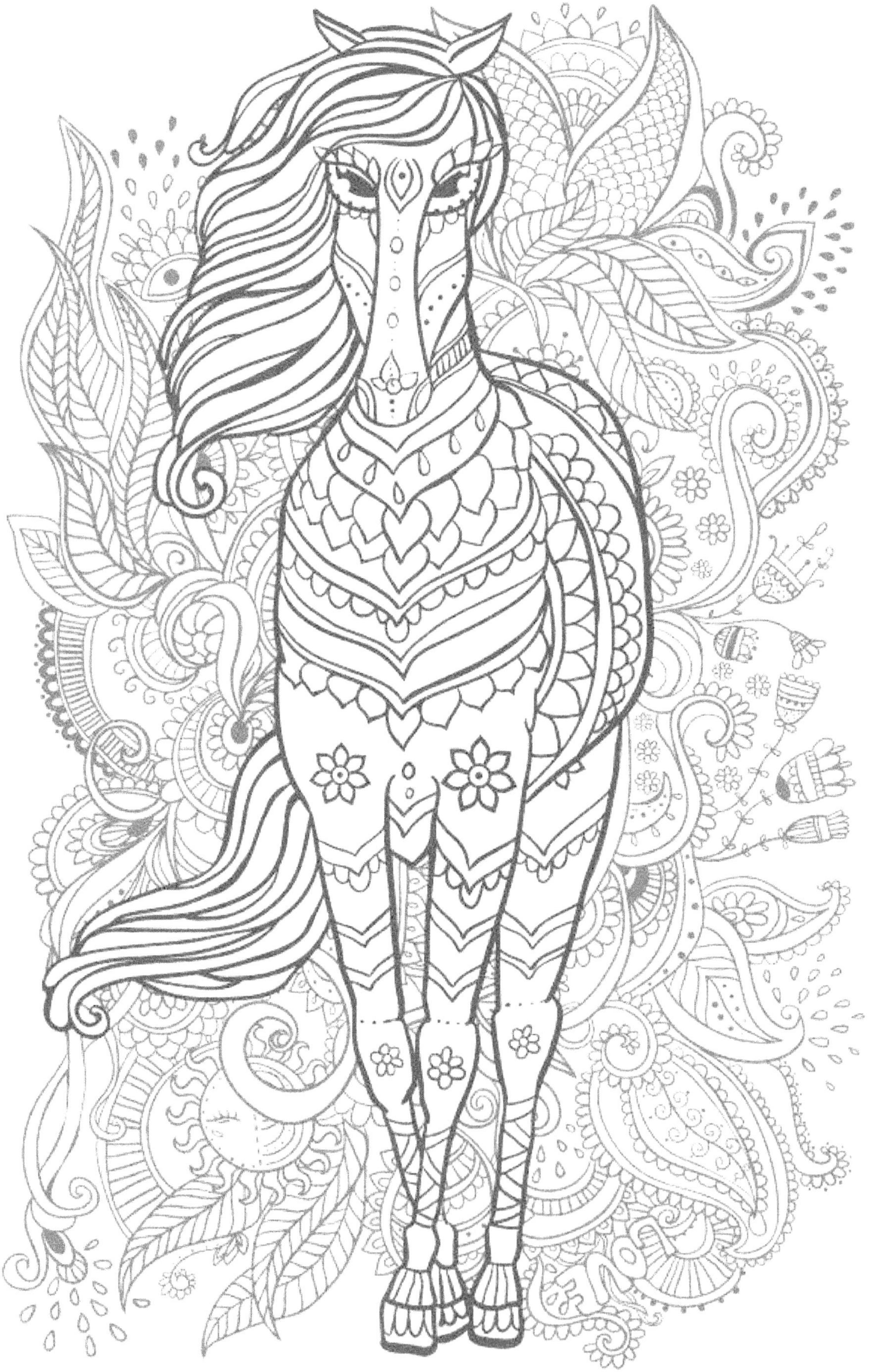

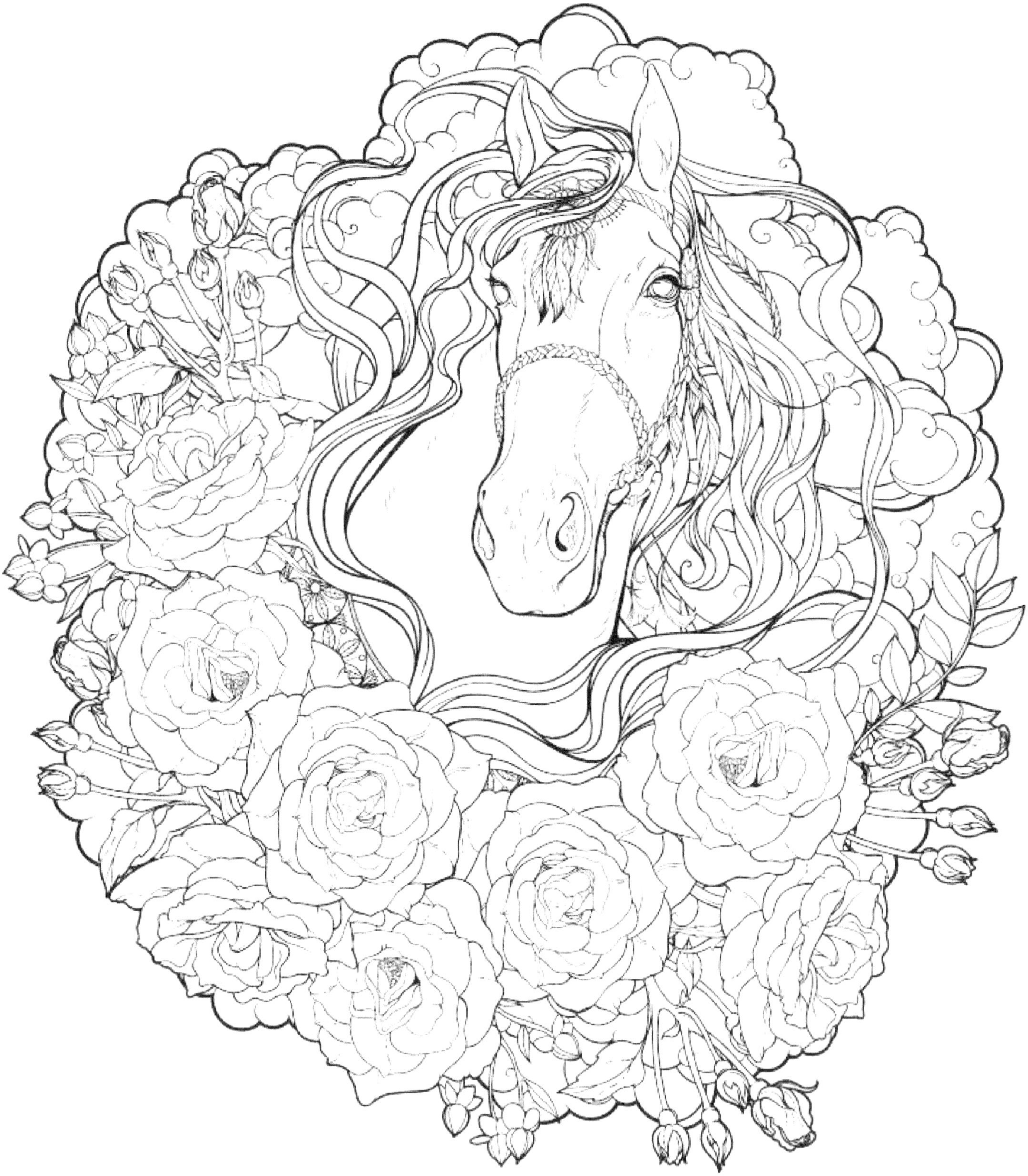

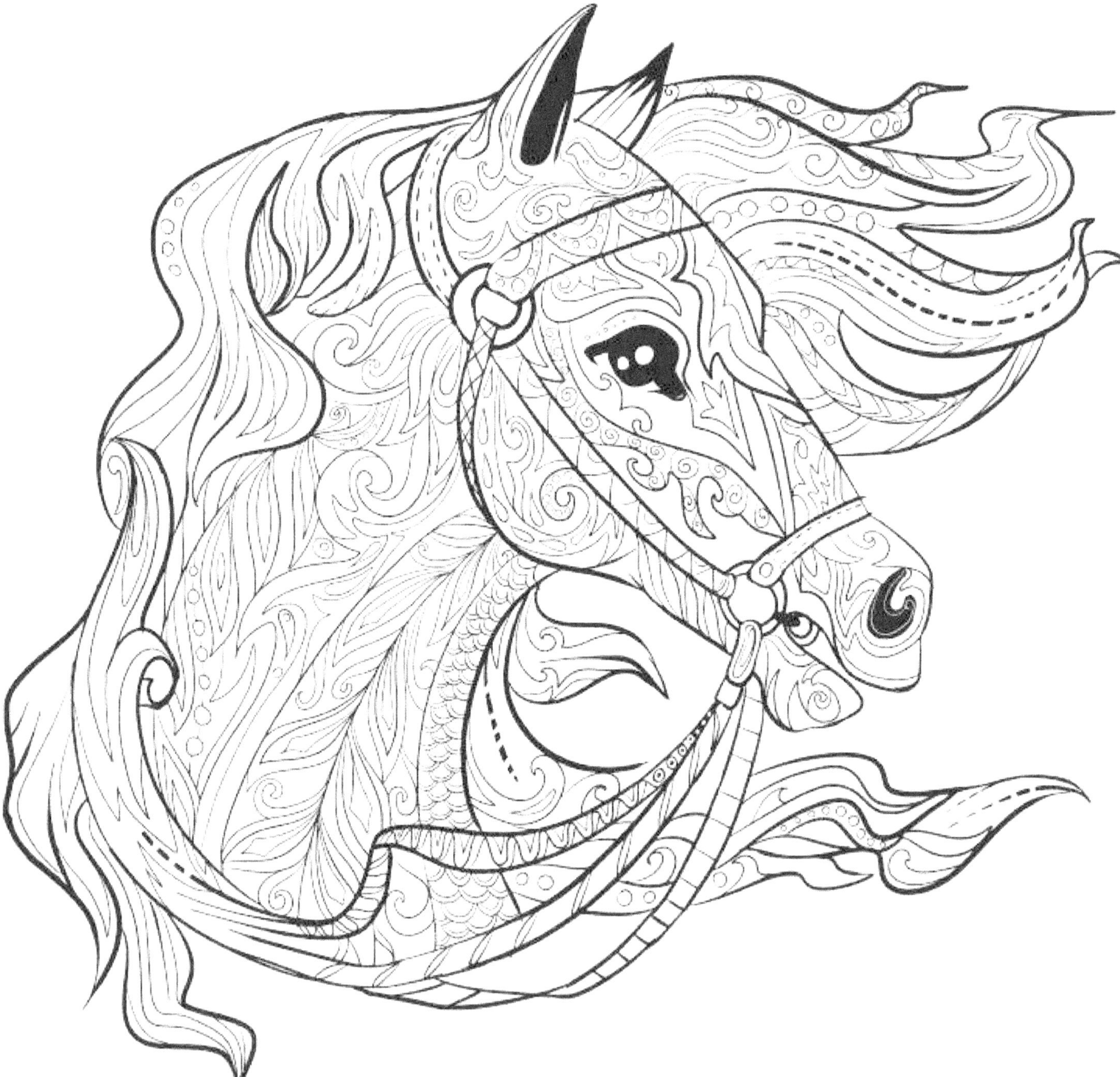

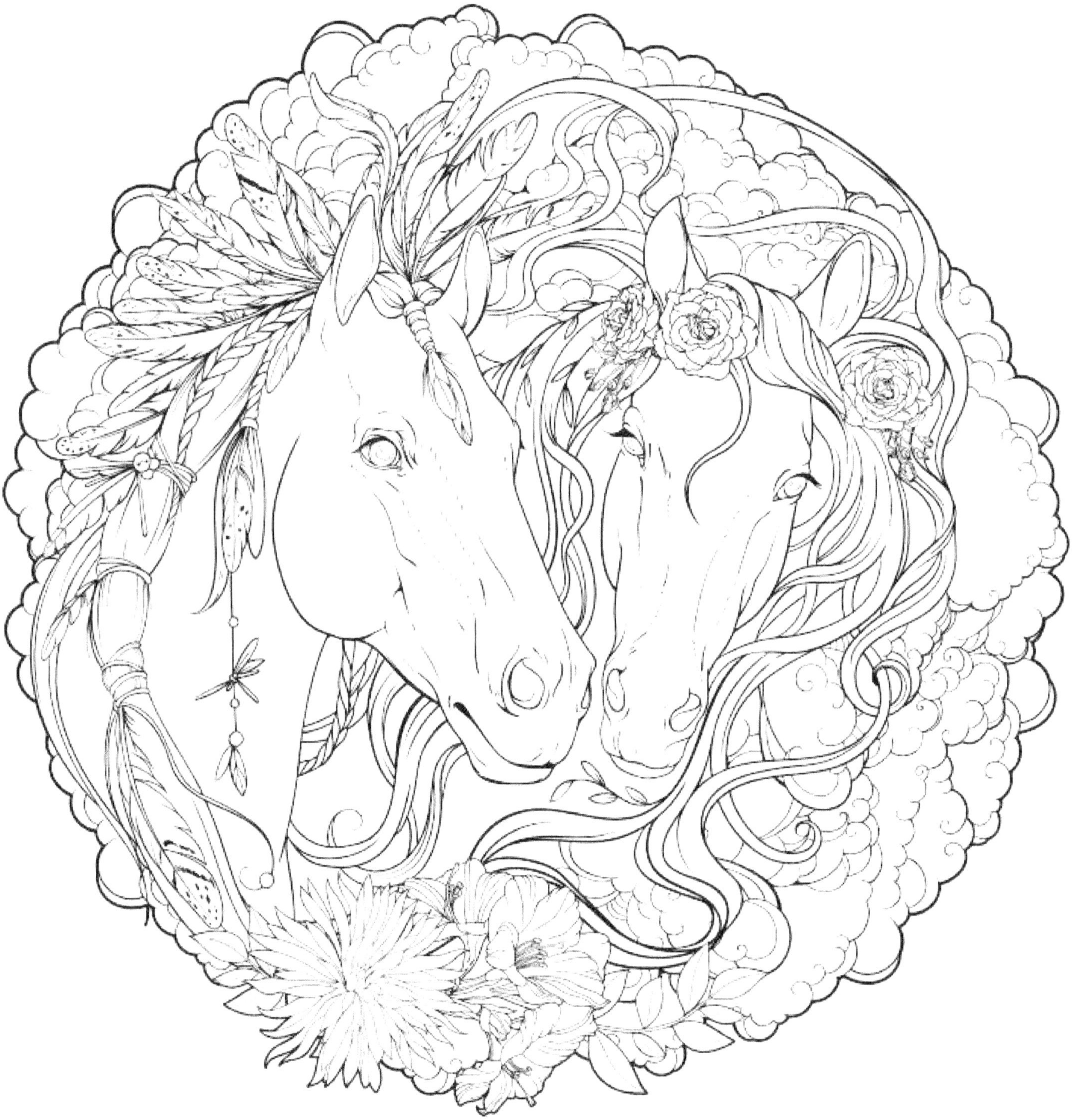

Bonus Hedgehogs and Turtles Coloring Pages to Enjoy!

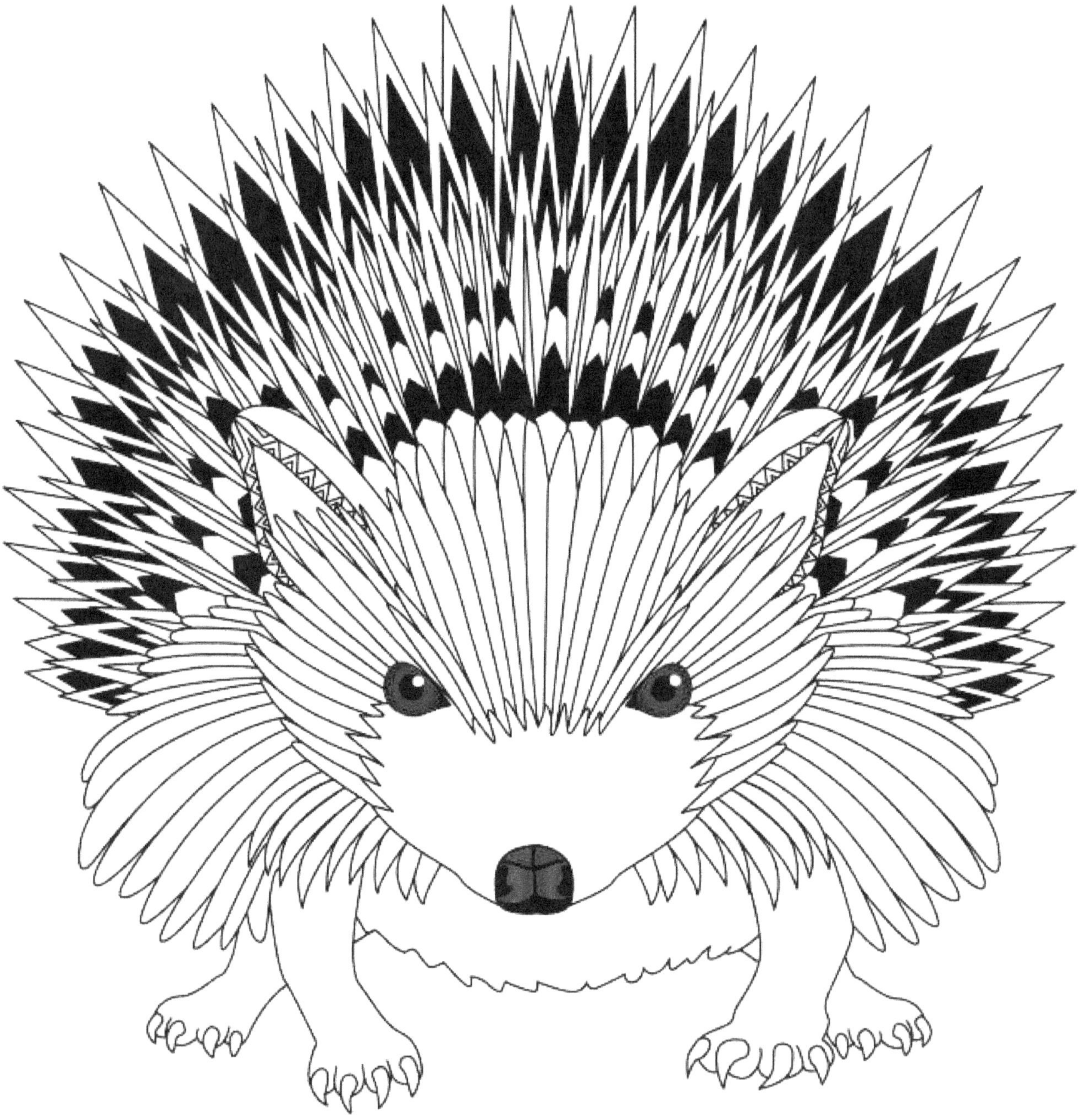

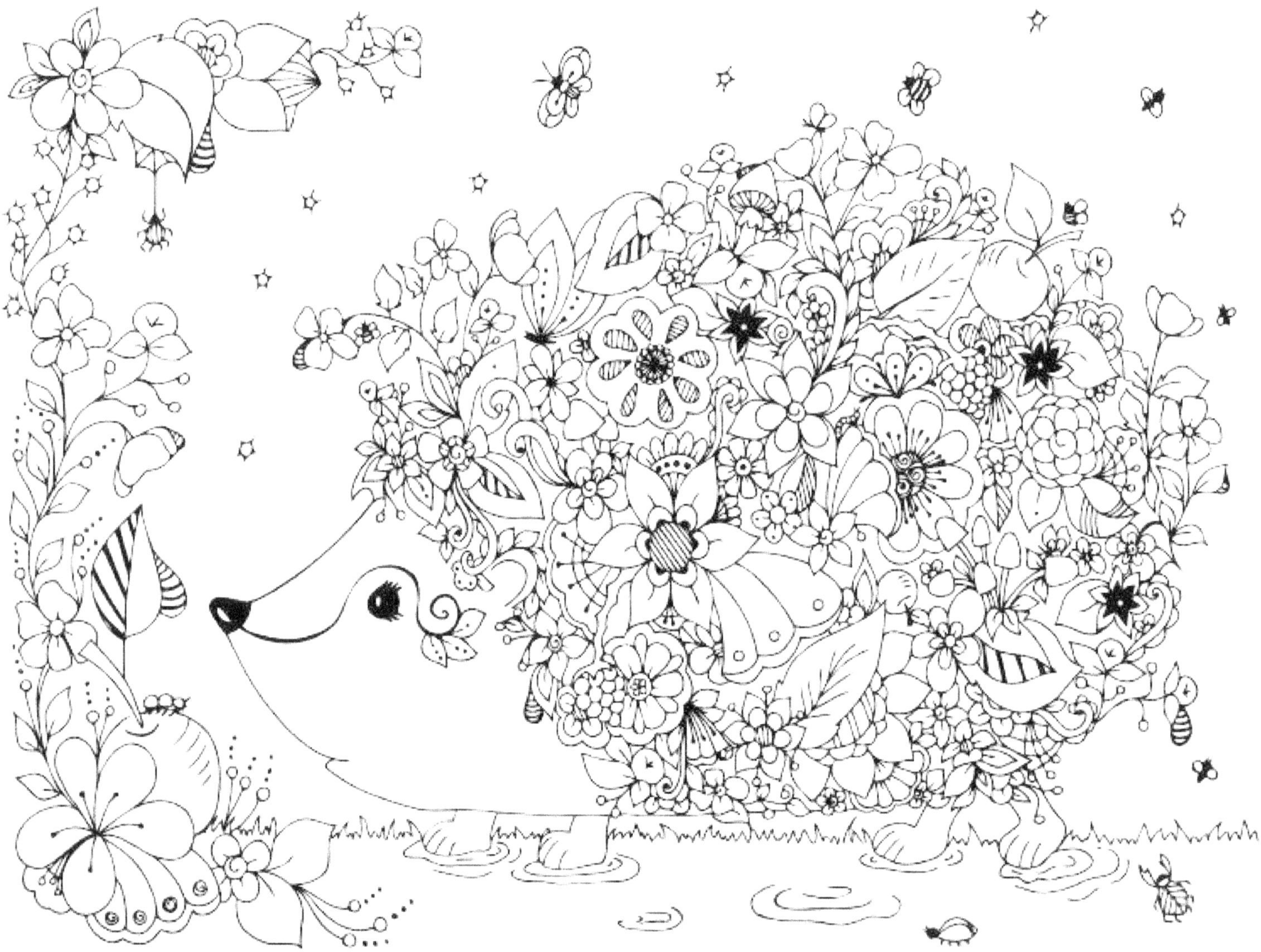

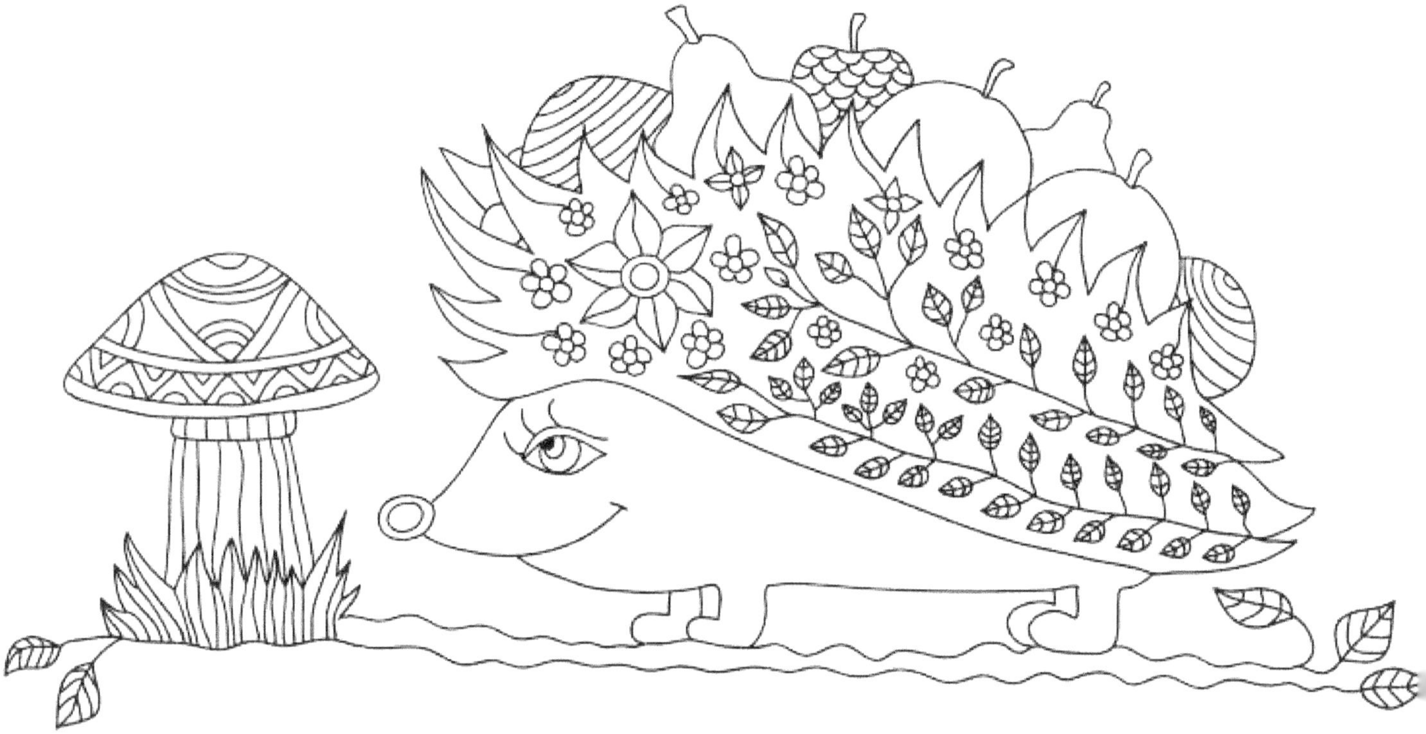

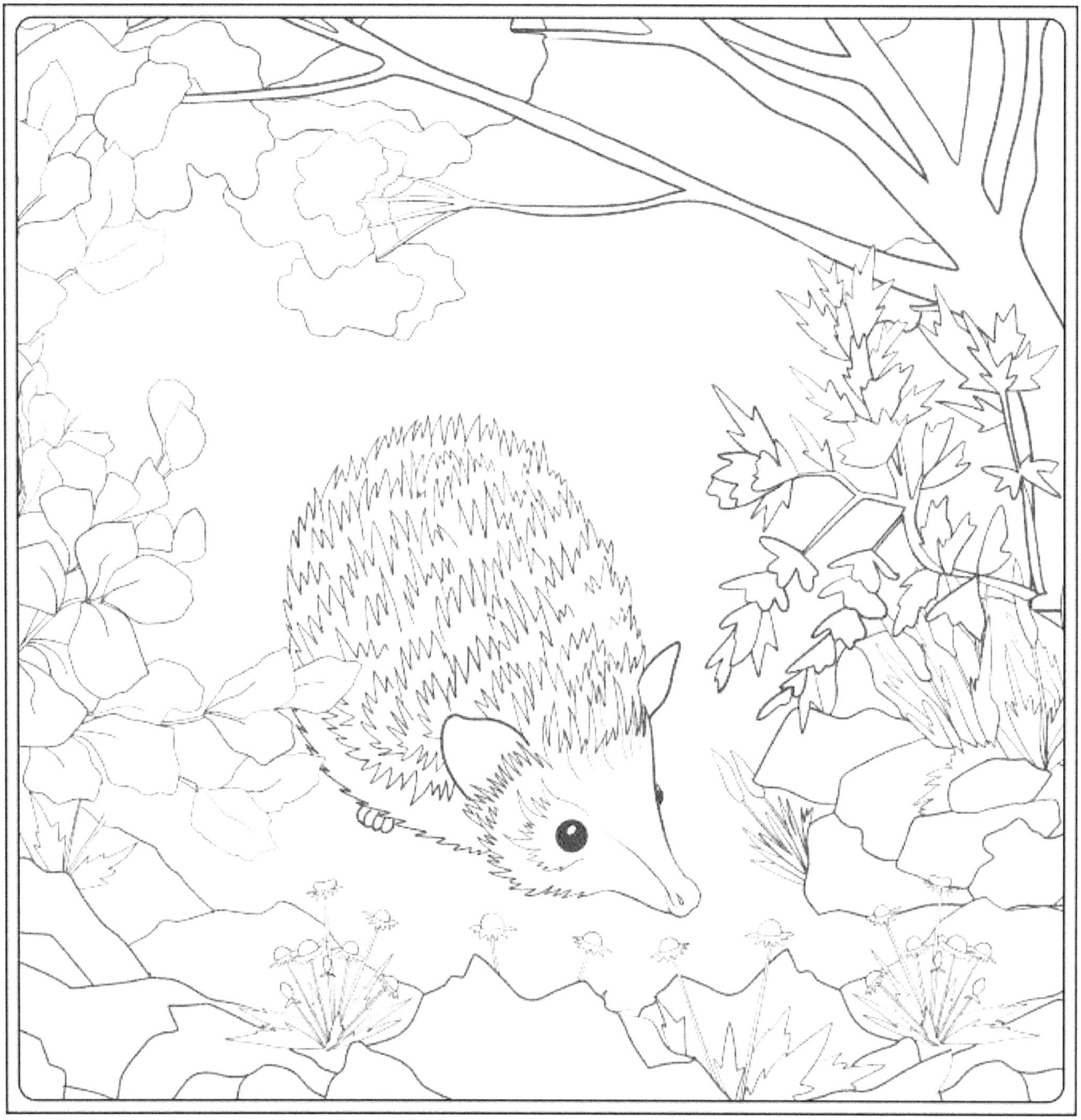

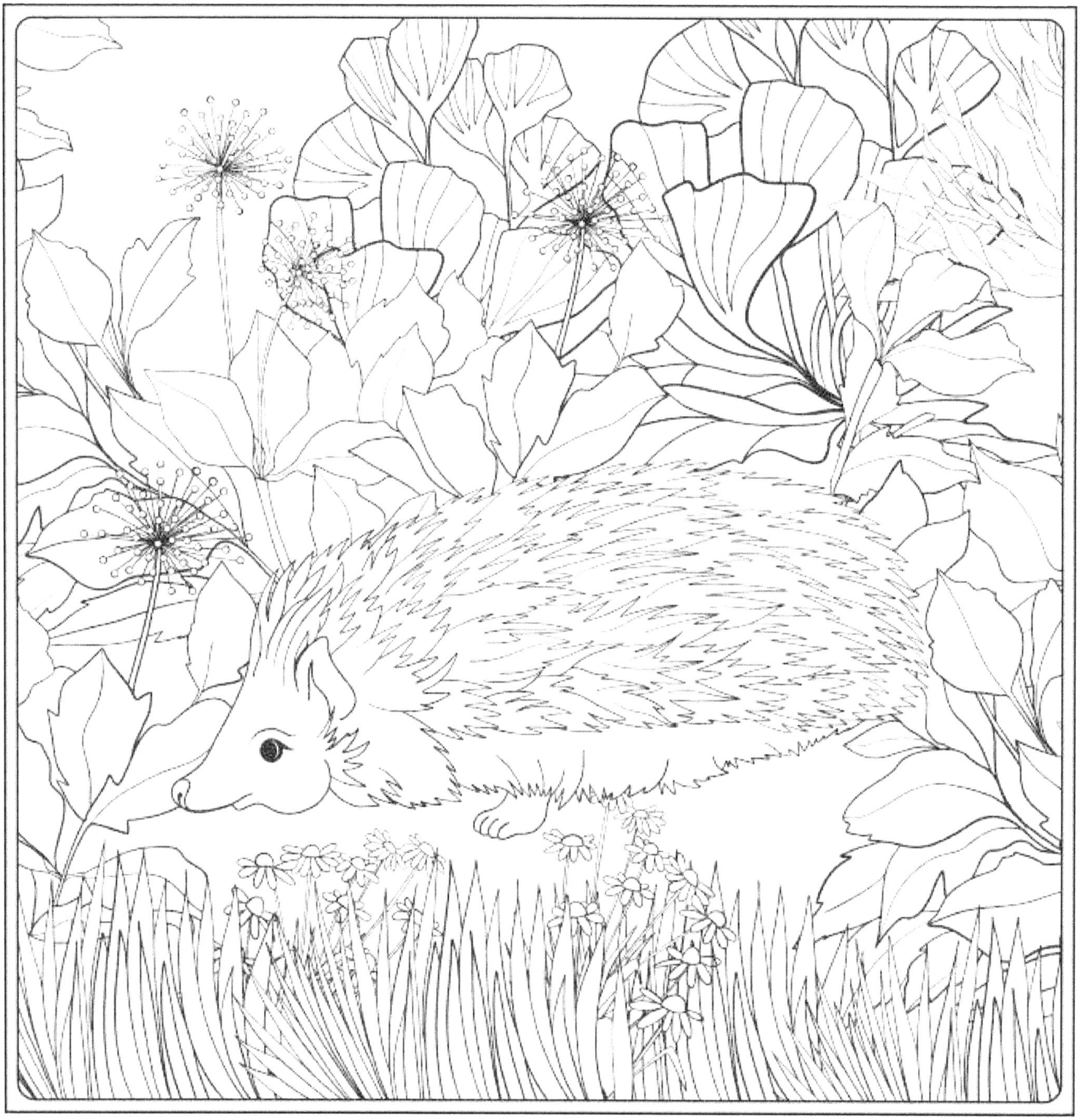

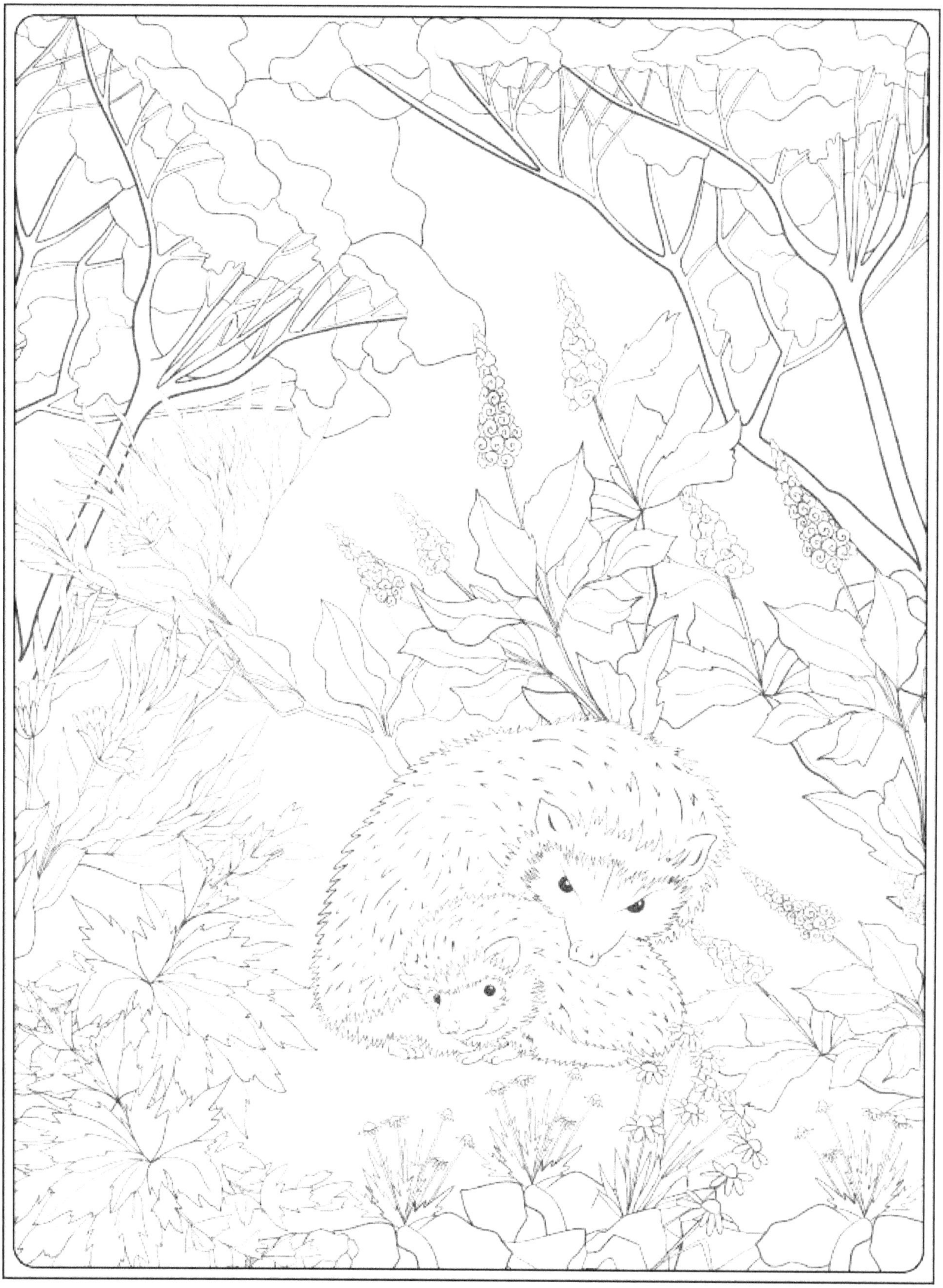

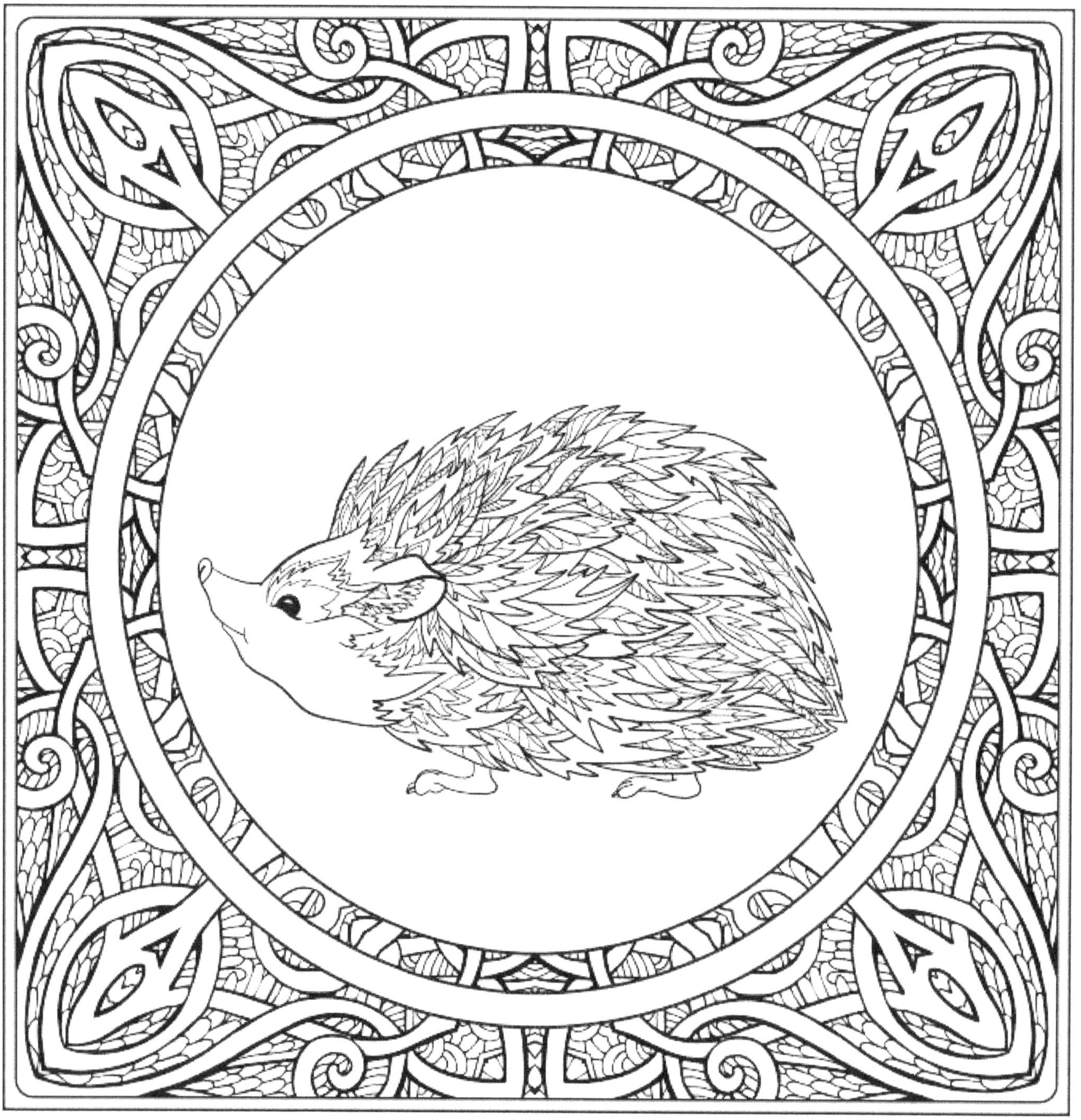

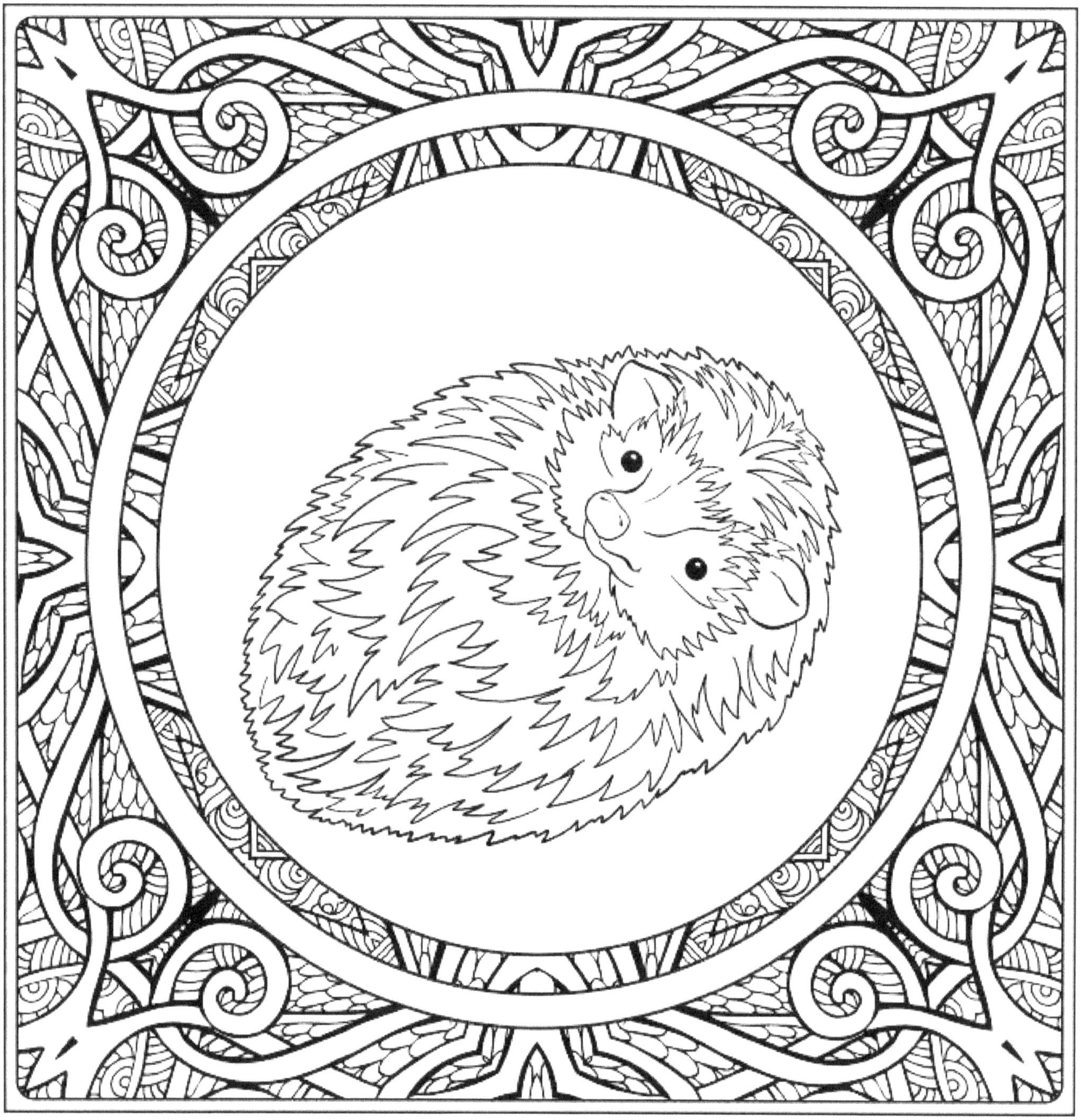

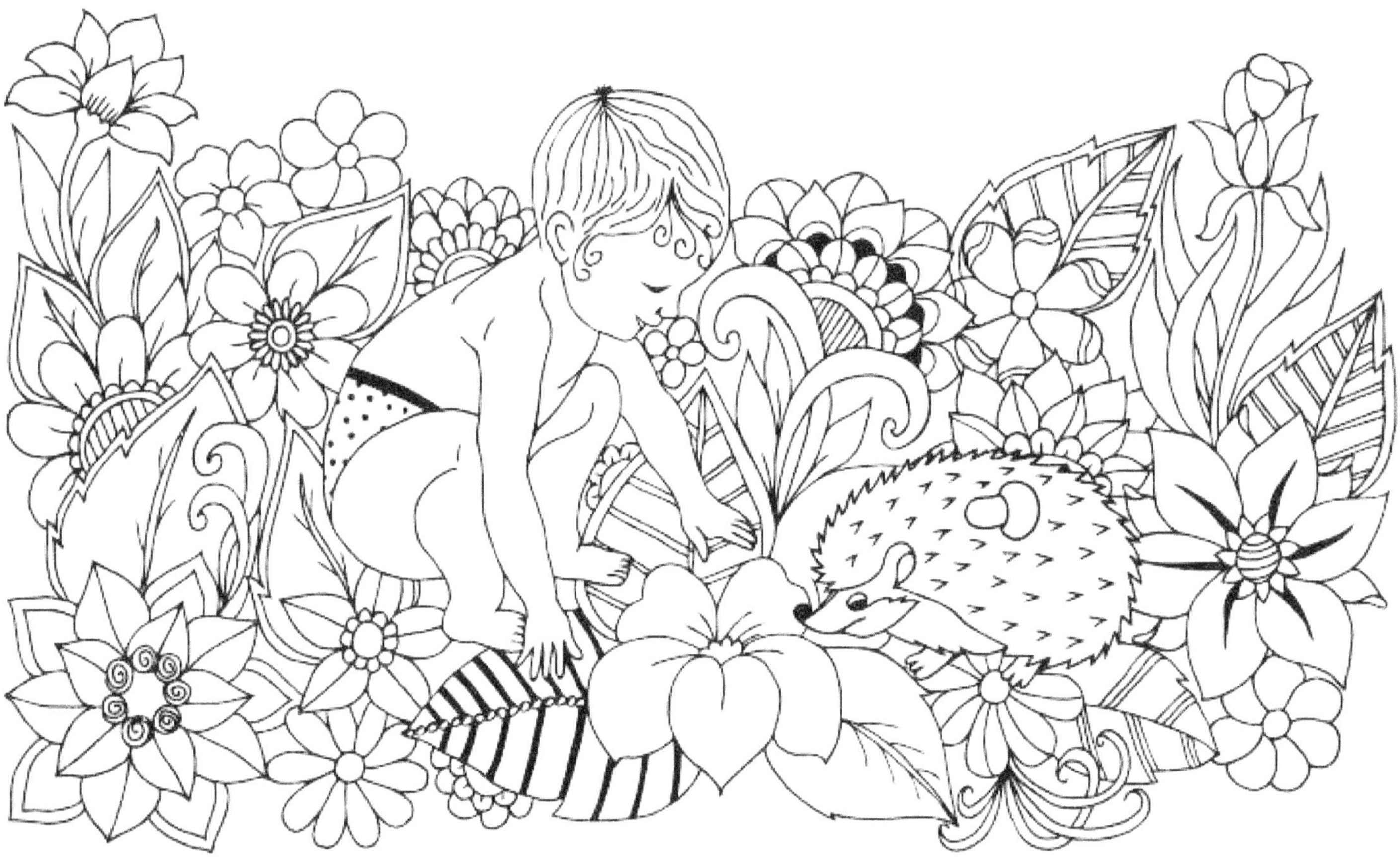

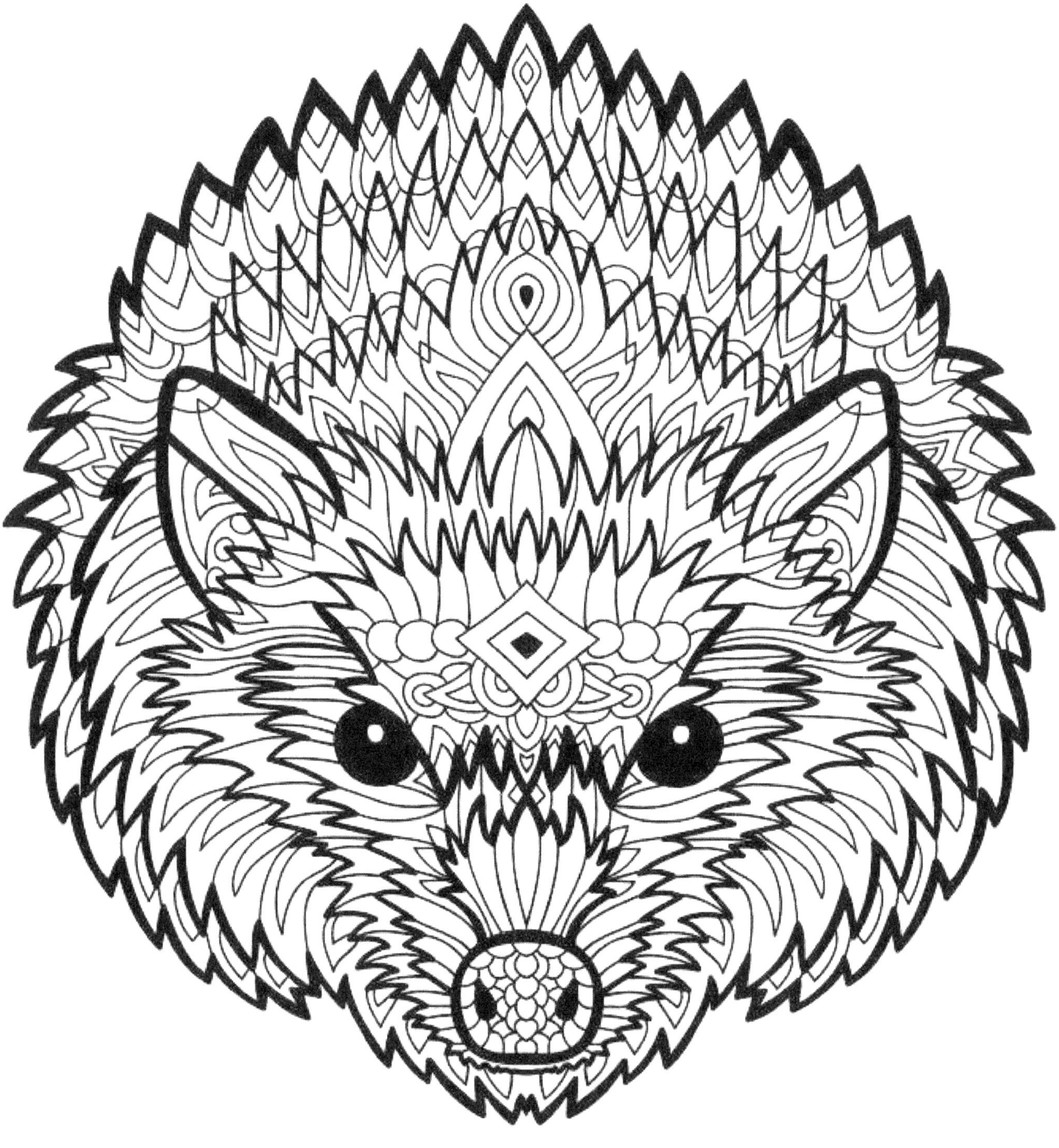

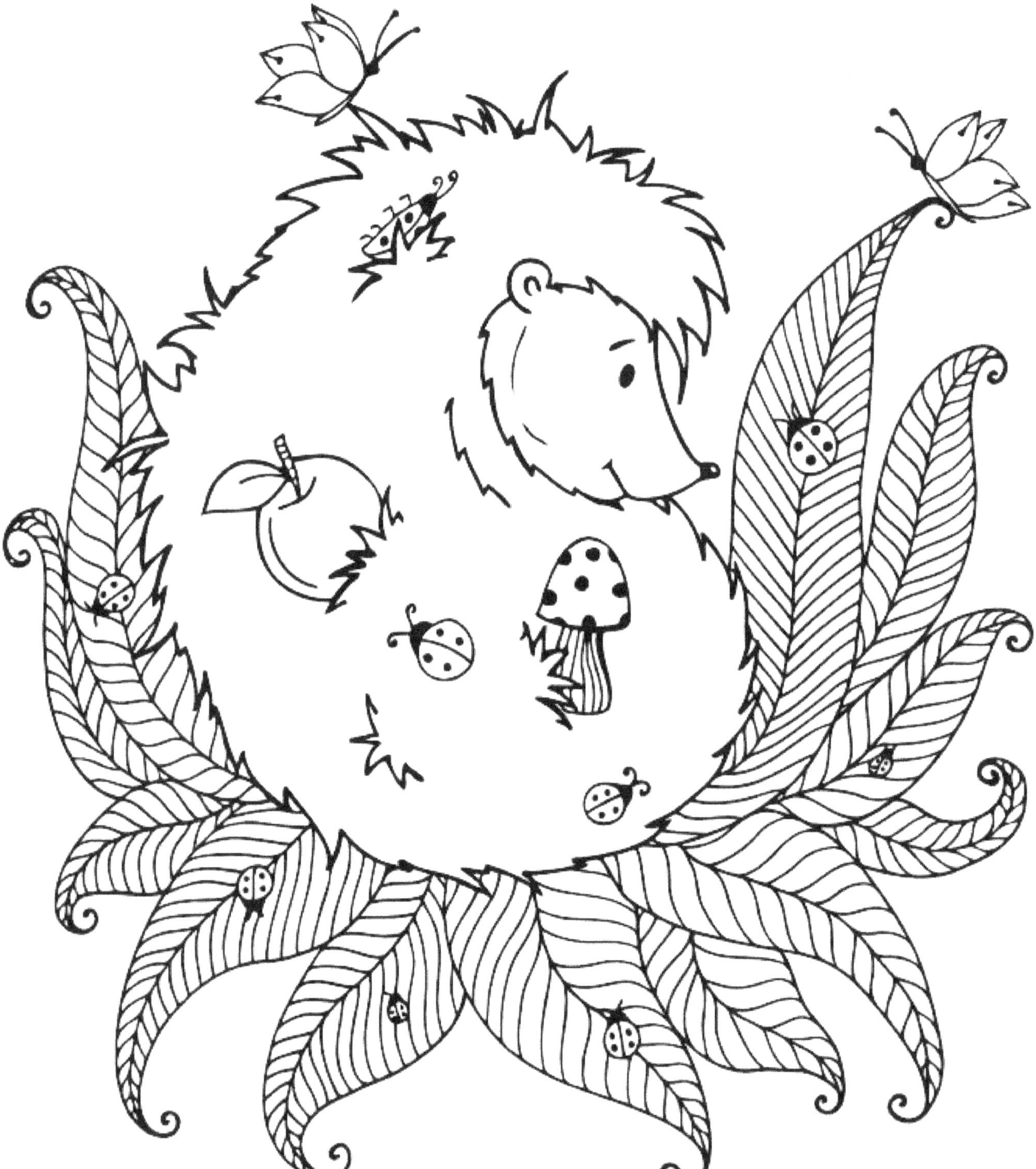

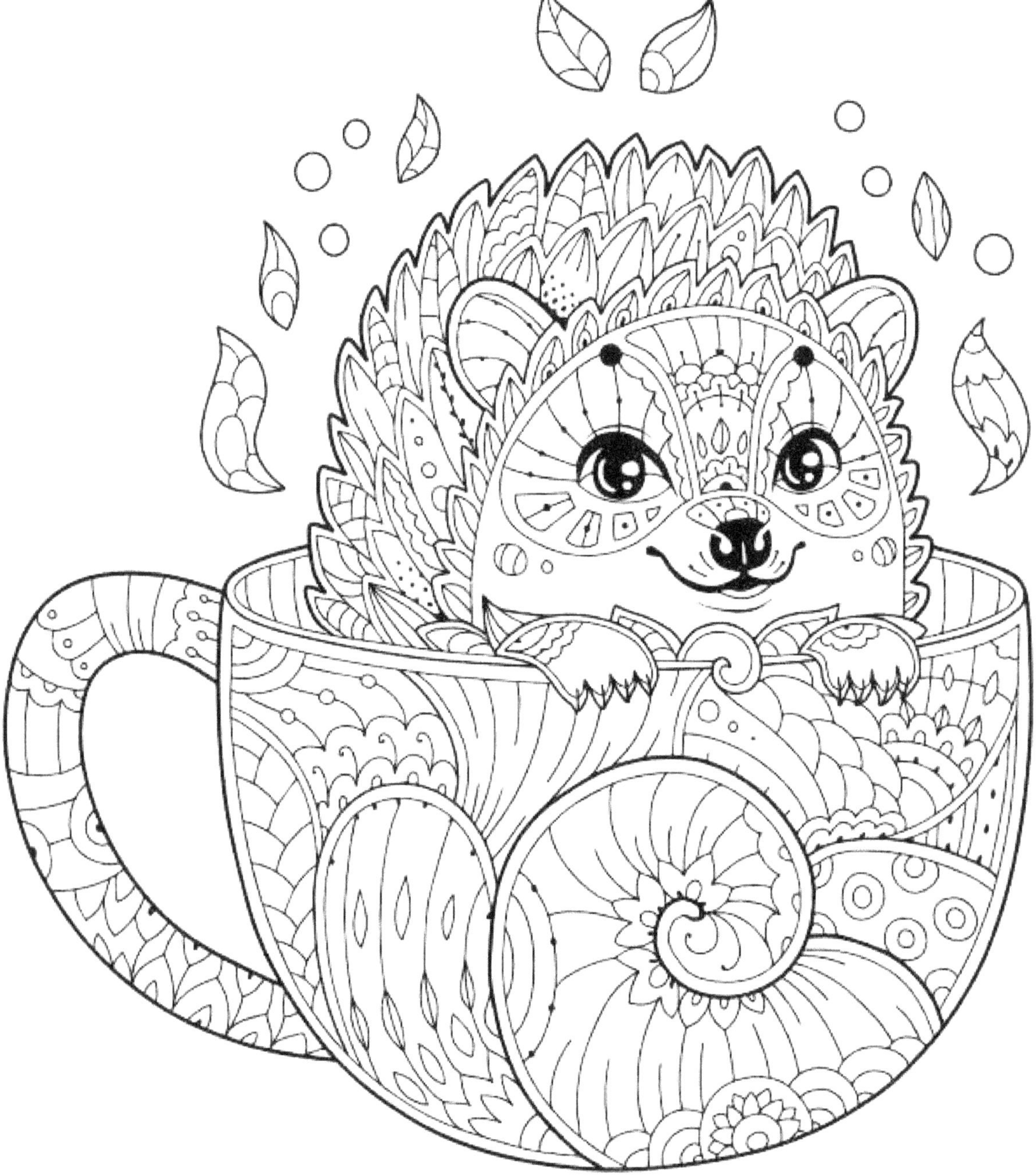

Surprise Bonus Turtle Coloring Illustrations for you to enjoy!

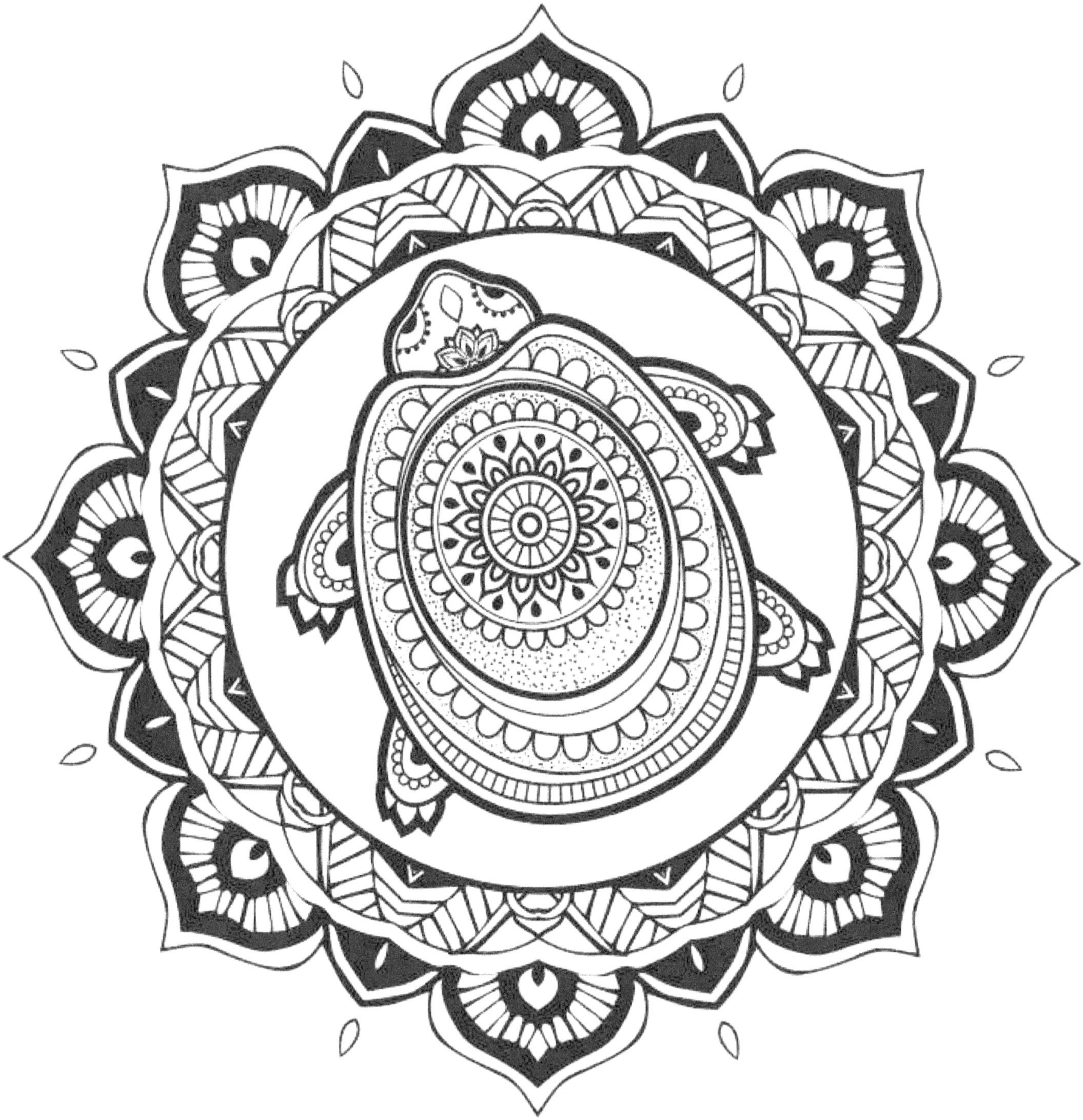

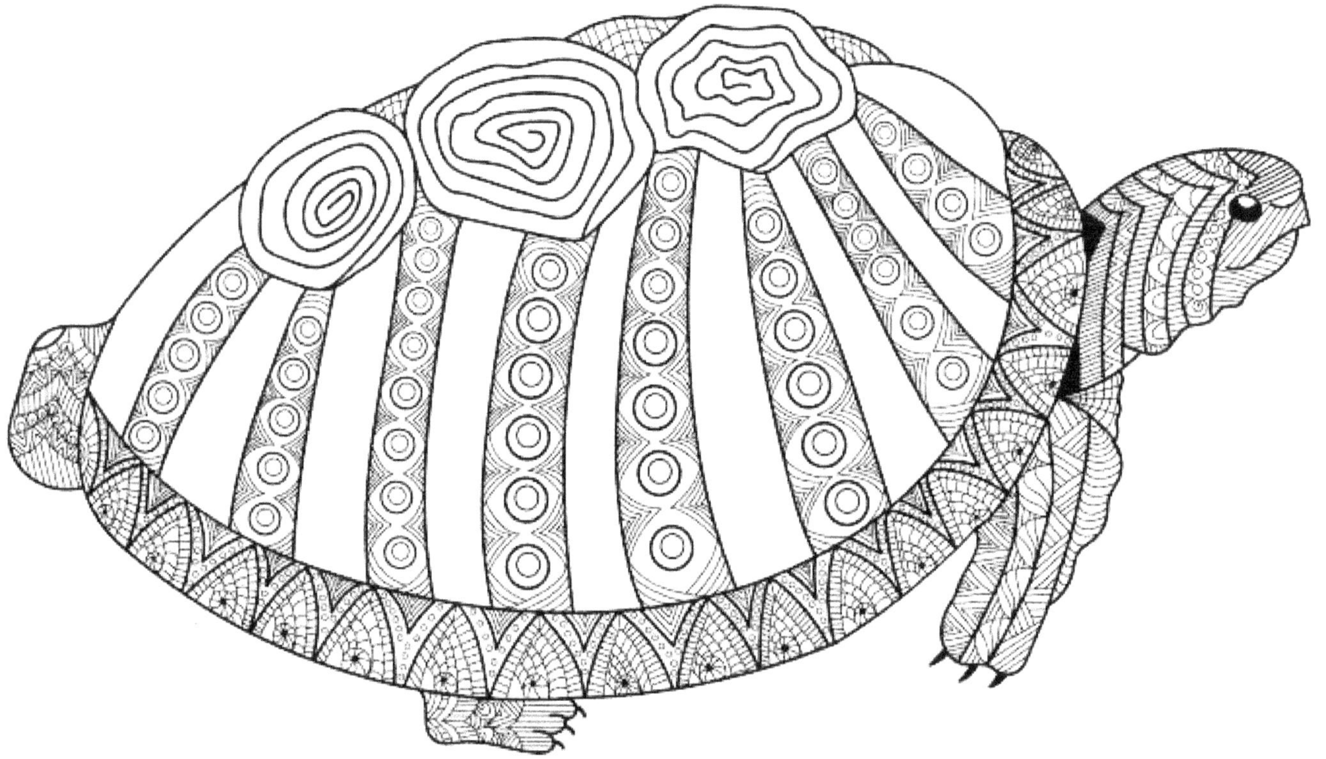

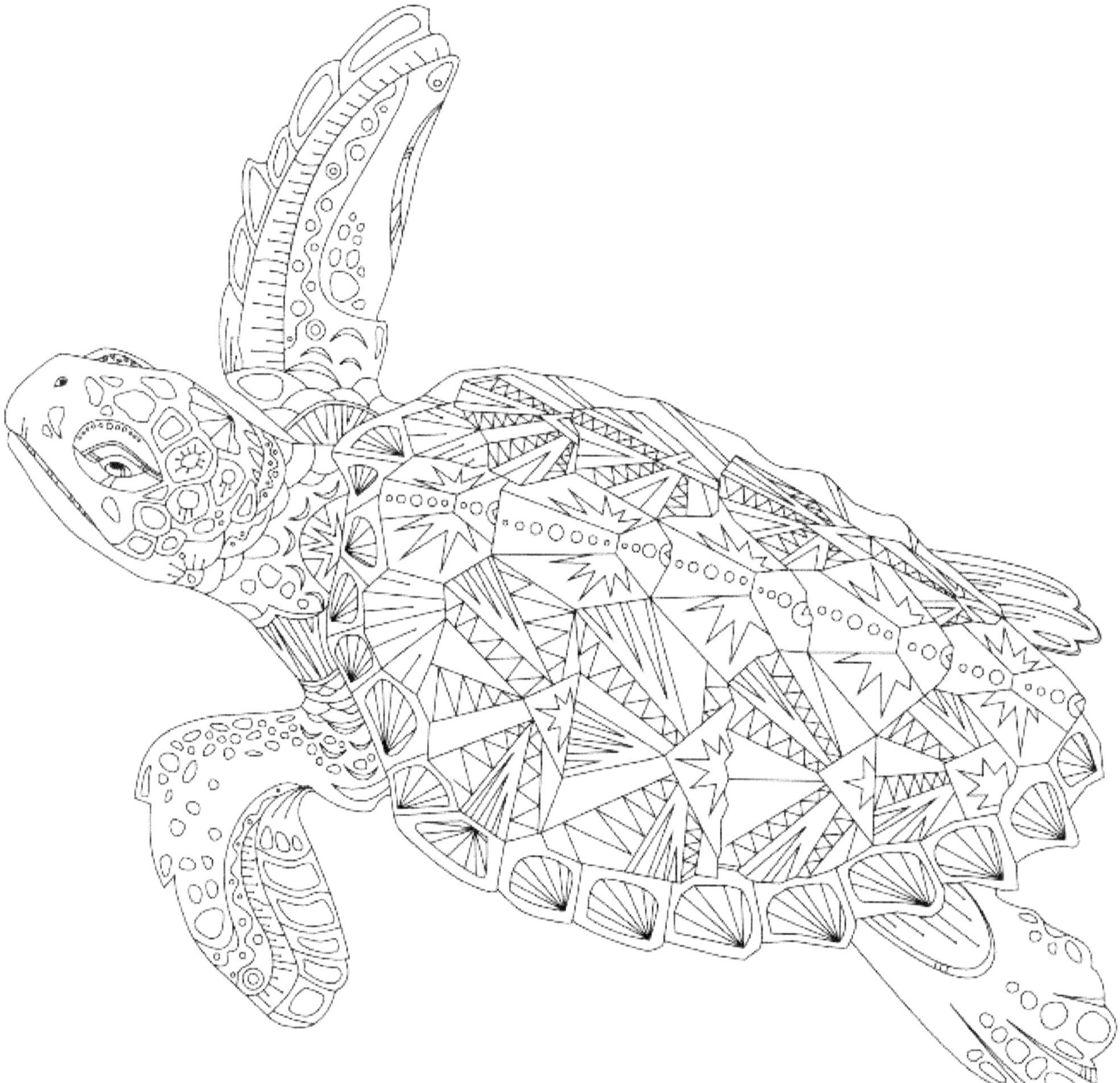

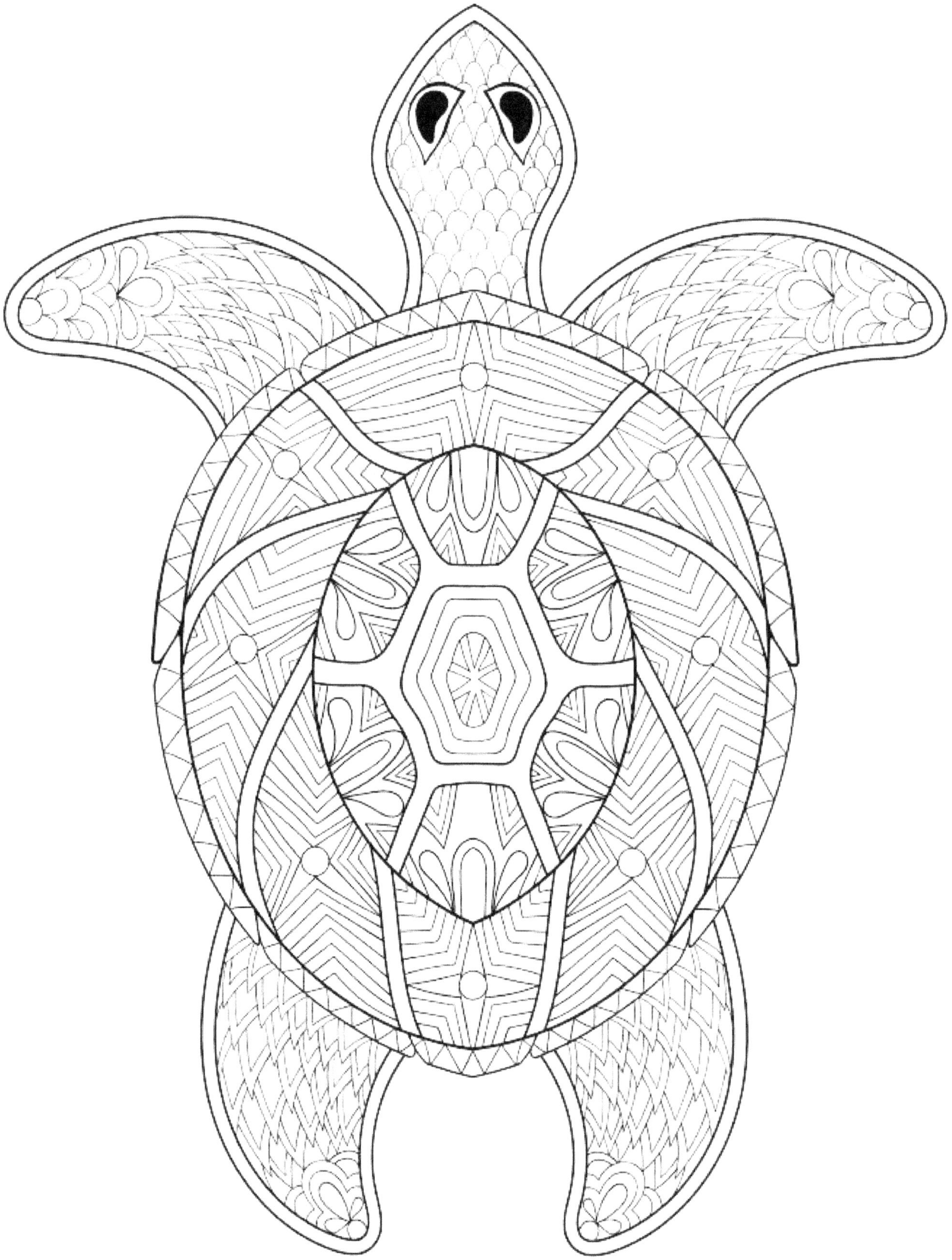

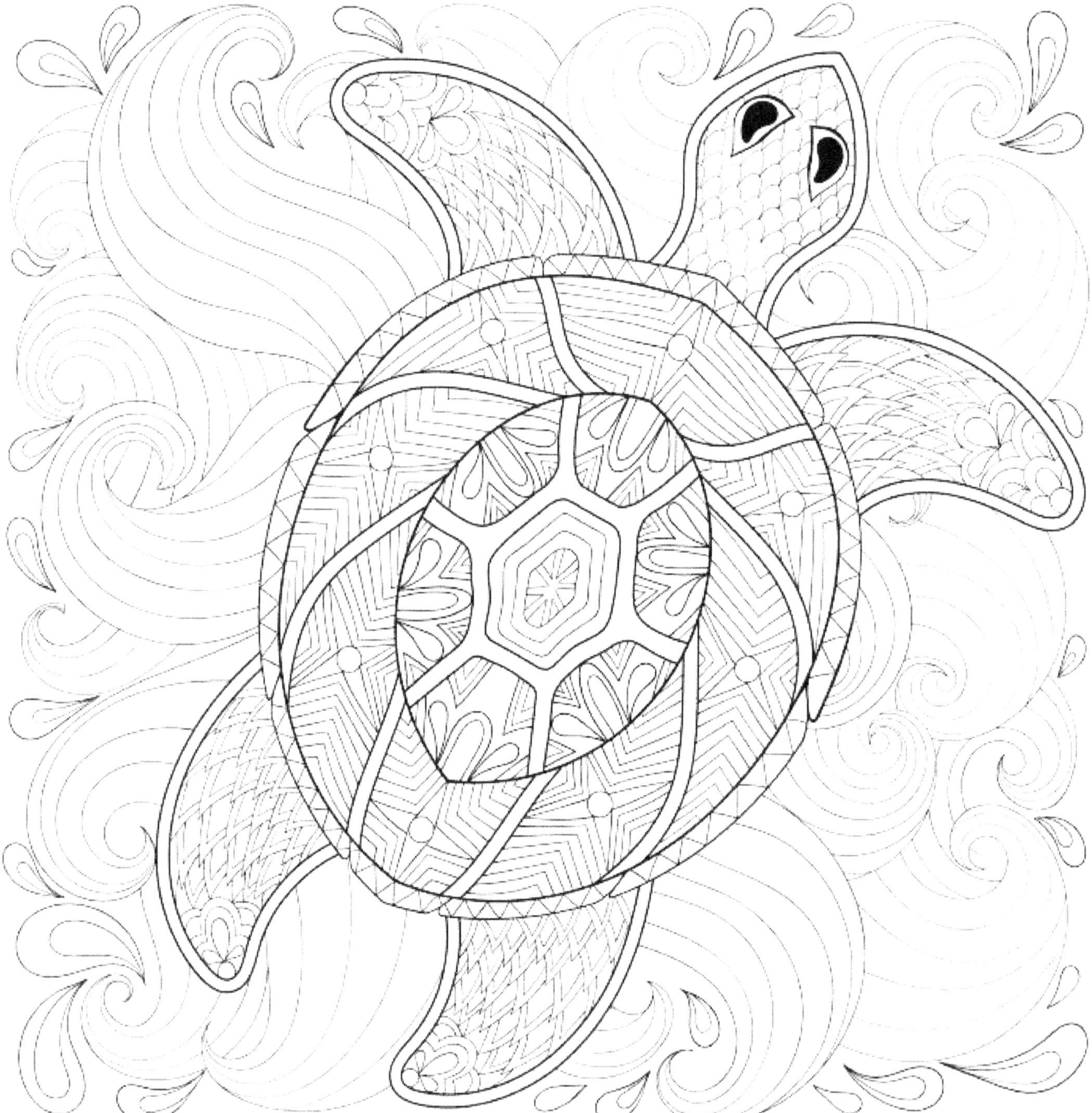

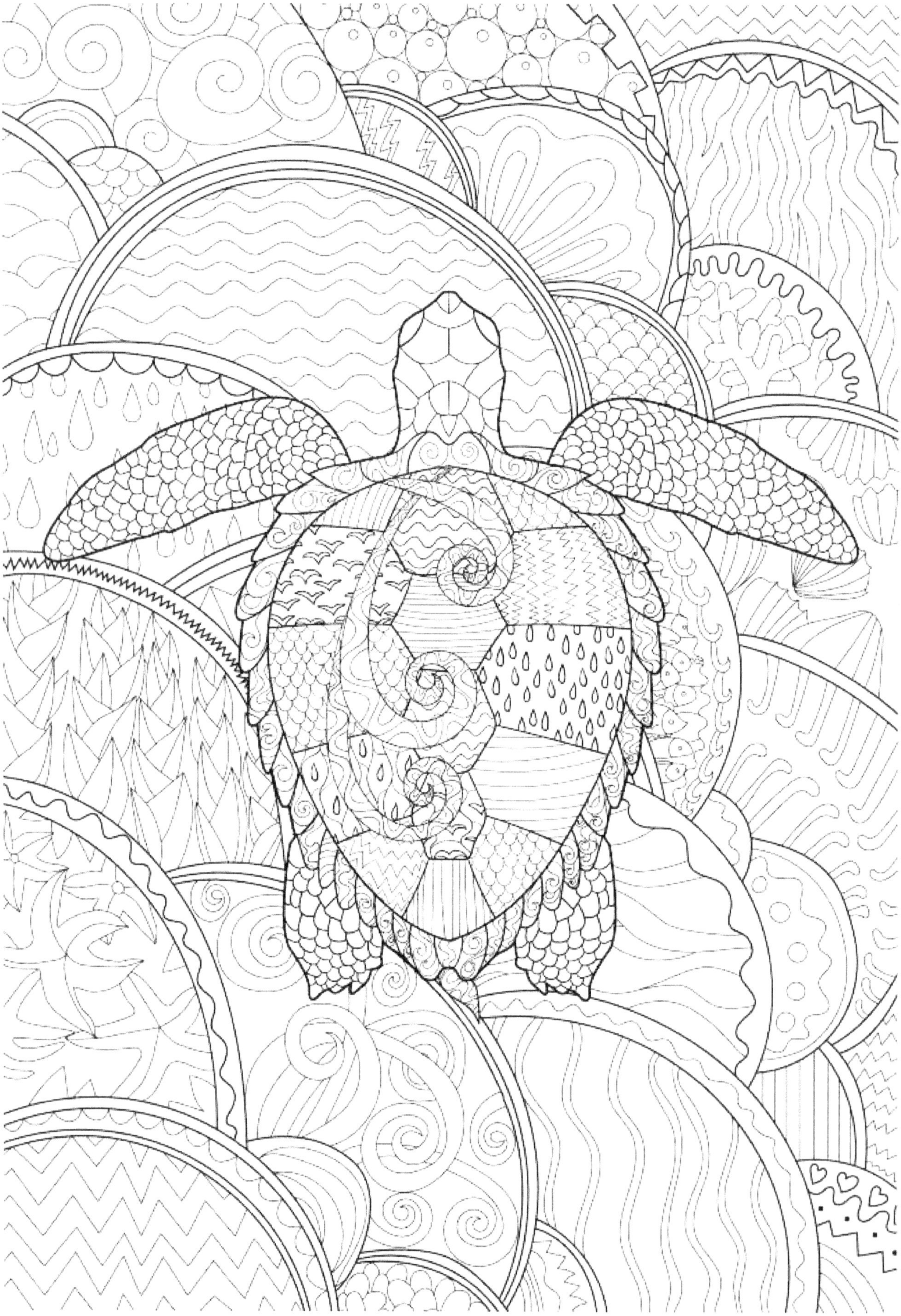

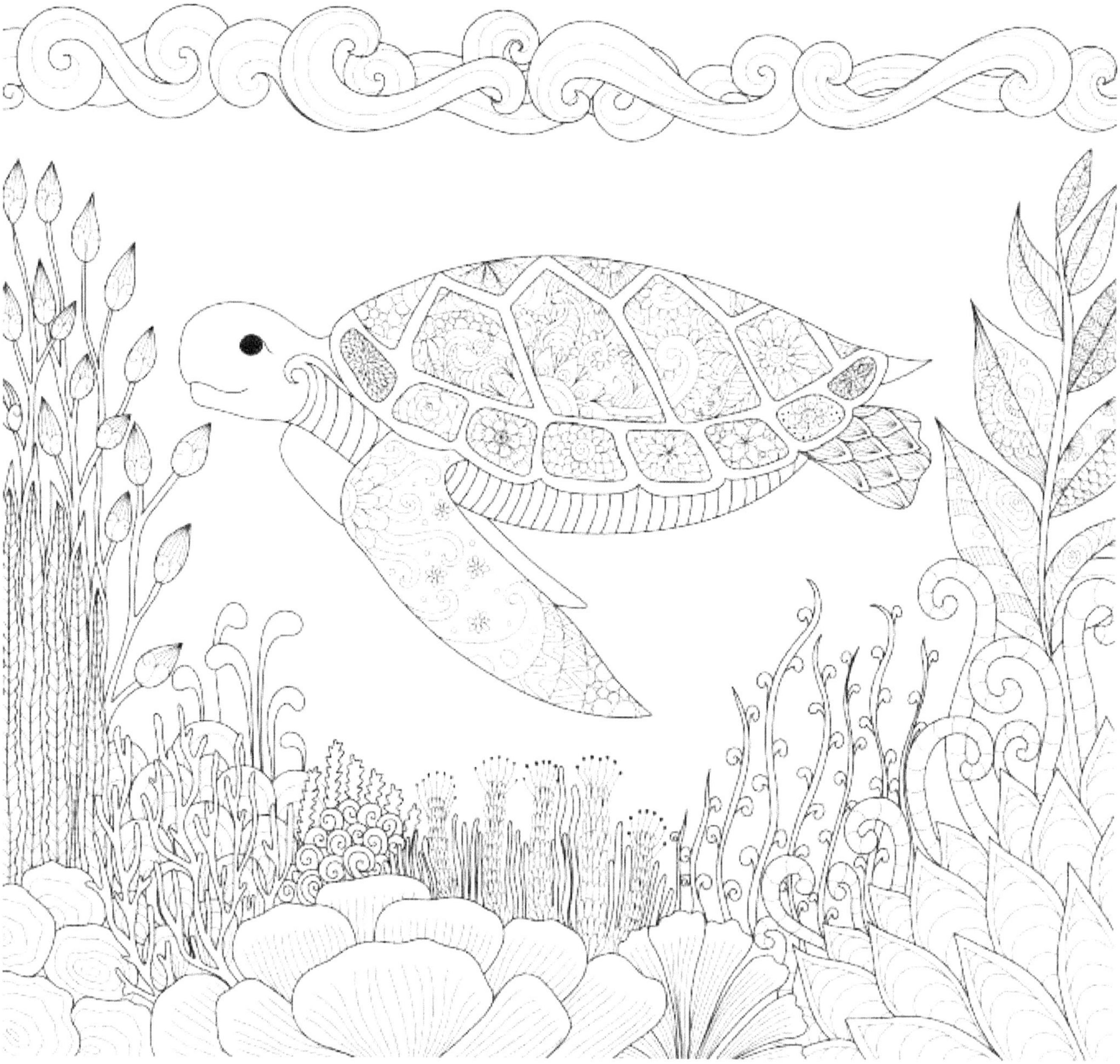

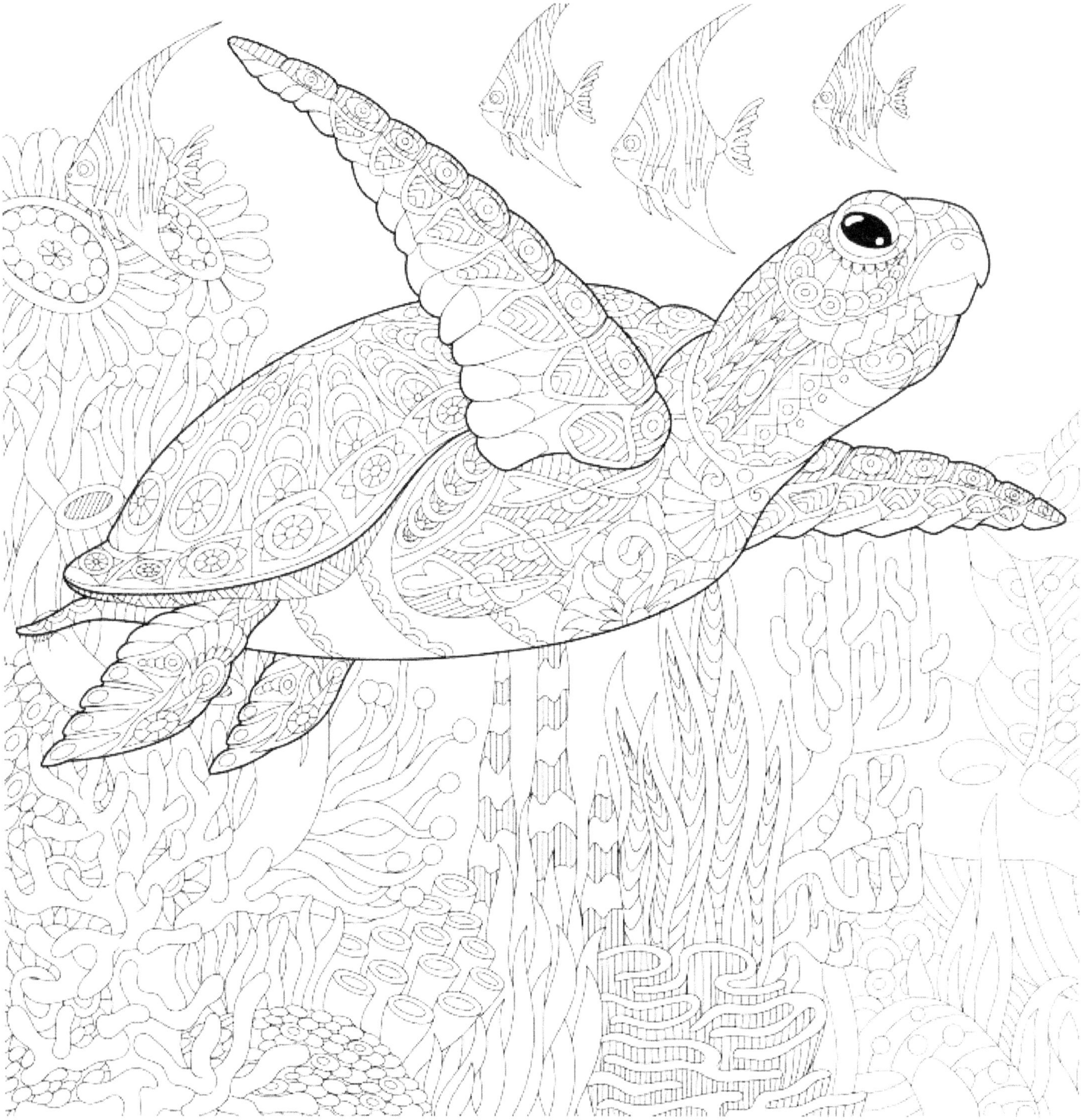

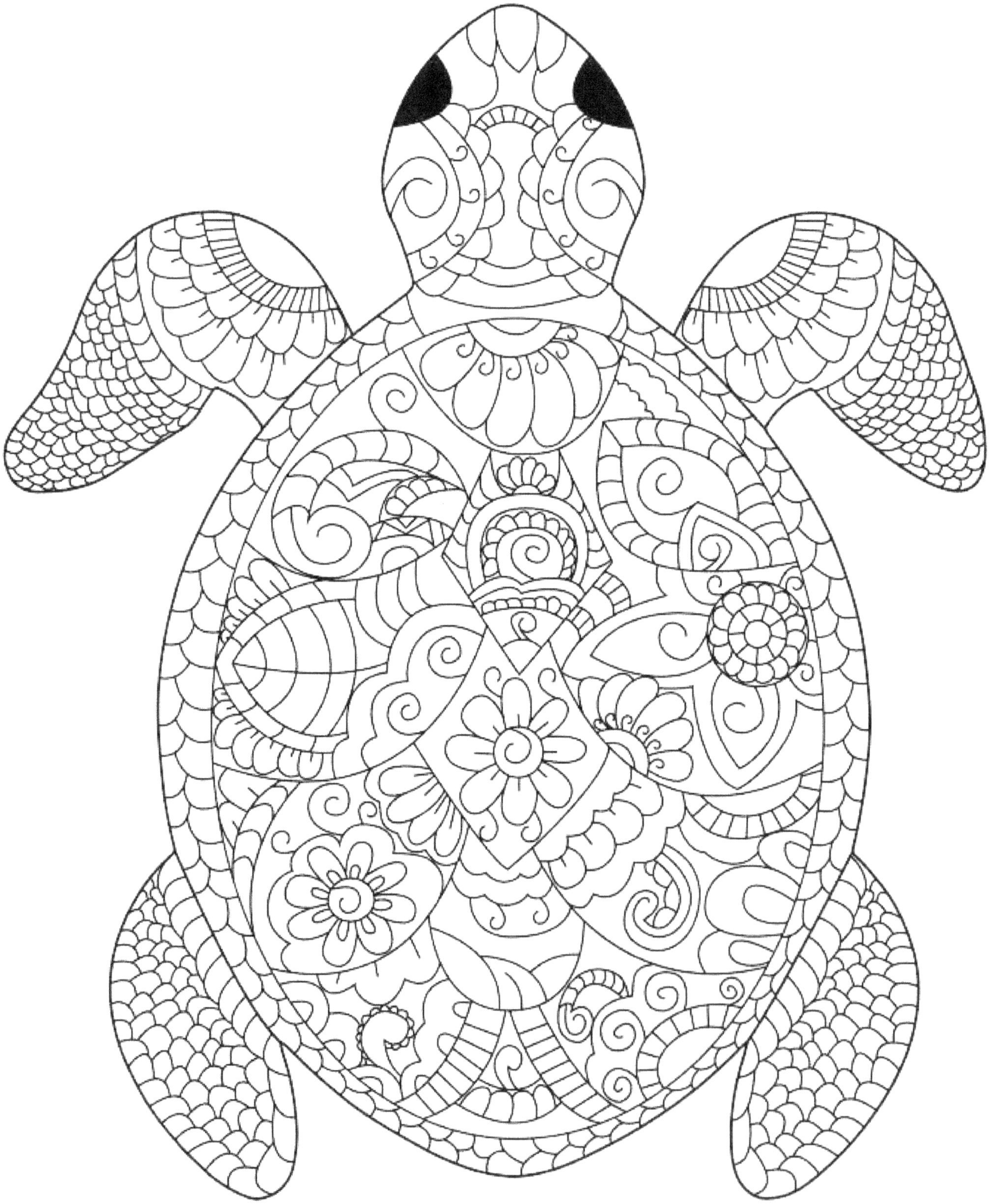

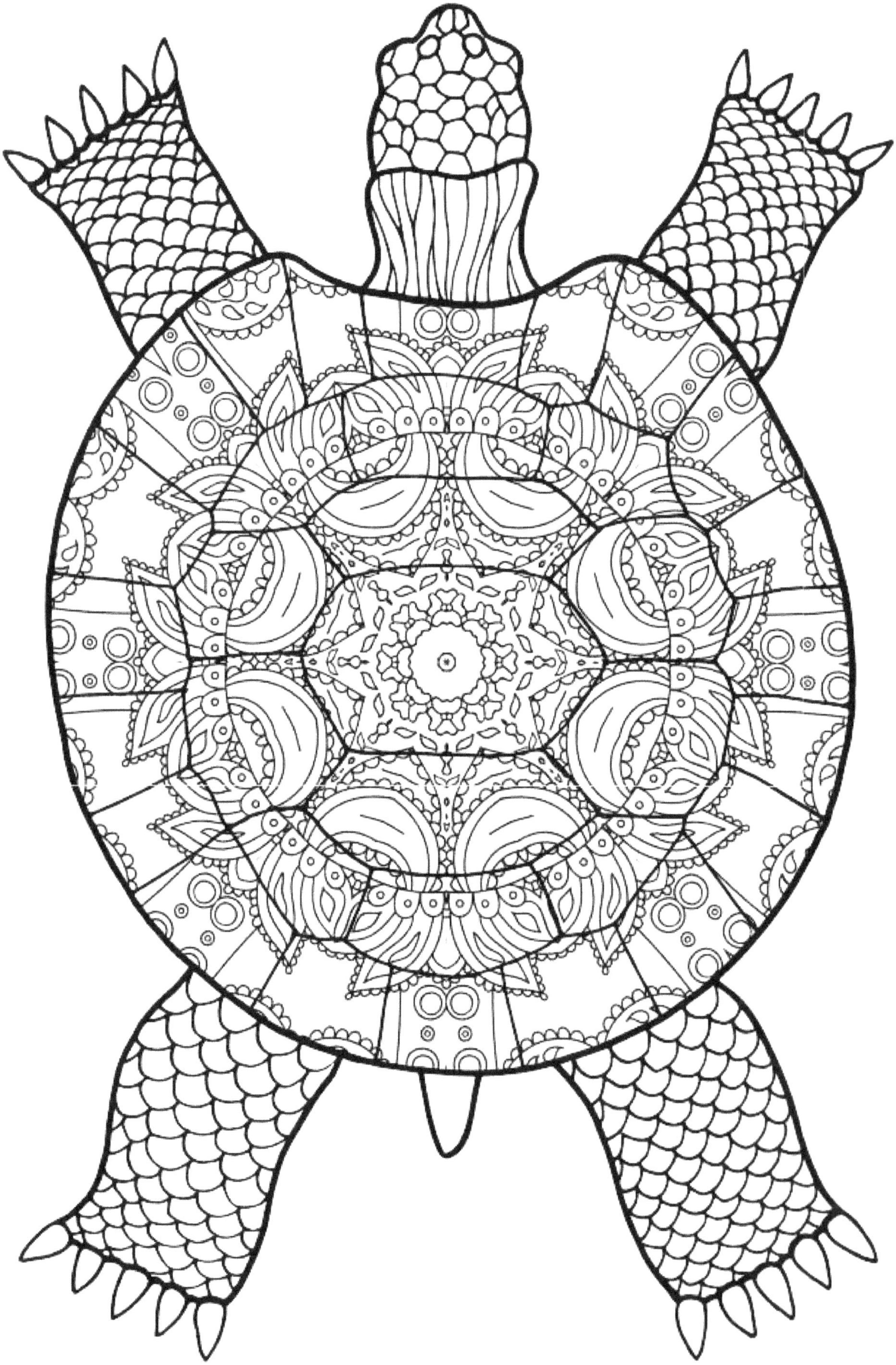

www.ingramcontent.com/pod-product-compliance
Lightning Source LLC
Chambersburg PA
CBHW081113180526
45170CB00008B/2826